GRACEFULLY

BROKEN

Antoinette D. Ranson

Unless otherwise indicated, all scripture references are from The King James Version of the Bible.

GRACEFULLY

BROKEN

Publishing assistance by:
R.R.H. Creation Printing & Publication Company
P.O. Box 800
Monee, IL. 60449
rrhcreation@gmail.com

Front & back cover designed by:
Loondon Graphiz/Photography
loondongraphiz@gmail.com

Copyright © 2021 by Antoinette D. Ranson

All rights Reserved.
No part of this publication may be reproduced, stored in a retrieval system, or transmitted in any form or by any means electronic, mechanical, photocopy, recording, or any other- except for brief quotations in print reviews, without the prior written permission of the author.

ISBN: 978-0-578-84439-8

GRACEFULLY

BROKEN

PRELUDE

In this book, "Gracefully Broken," we will navigate some personal journeys that I have traveled, which I experienced some of the most challenging experiences in my life. Many Christians are facing daunting life situations that may have made them feel like throwing in the towel. When issues seem impossible, it might be challenging to see the light at the end of the tunnel. You might find yourself asking the question, "Why do I seem to be going through so much?" This book is designed to share my journey from being gracefully broken to being made whole. The book is intended to bring healing and deliverance to others who have experienced brokenness. Divorce, the death of a loved one, overlooked for a promotion, or even hurt in the church, are broken areas that affect us in many ways. God allows us to experience crushing, like the olive, to produce a sweet-smelling aroma and bring out things in us that we have yet to discover. Jesus asked a question in

GRACEFULLY BROKEN

John 5:6, *"Wilt thou be made whole?"* The truth of the matter is that you can be made whole. When a glass is shattered, some pieces are too small to see with the naked eye. The intricate pieces that are not seen with the naked eye, might not be required to put the damaged areas back together. Let God put the pieces together.

FOREWORD
Pastor Capatoria Wilson

I sauntered down the lane, from the street to the gargantuan building, following my grandmother to a place I had never known. My life before had been lived-in a three-story courtyard building where everyone knew each other, in fact, we were all family. Our entire family had been displaced because of the expansion of a high school. No one asked us how we felt about moving. I was about eight years old at that time. I did the only thing I knew how to do, the only thing I had been taught to do, "follow my grandmother." I walked behind her, trying to follow the very footsteps she took. This was so unfamiliar to me, even scary. My family moved from a neighborhood where there were three to four-story apartment buildings. As I looked up, I noticed these buildings were much taller. The buildings were nine-stories in height. If that was not bad enough, some were connected. I was so afraid, and I did not know what to expect as we walked down the lane towards our new home.

I looked at the front of the building that would become my new address 2320 South State. I saw a little girl standing there. She was pretty, but most of all she was friendly. She welcomed me to the neighborhood as if she were sent there to ease my mind of my uncertain future. Her smile decreased the size of the building and lit up the sky. Like the sun, she melted my scary, frigid heart and warmed my world, over fifty-two years ago. She would later become "MY OLDEST FRIEND IN THE WORLD." Her name, Antoinette Denise Ranson, the author of the book you now hold in your hand.

I have had the honor of closely observing the mountain top experiences and the valley lows that Antoinette meticulously navigates while being "Gracefully Broken." This journey, which she transparently exposes, reminds us that we all go through. She gives us tools to help us evolve from those experiences. I sat enthralled as I turned the pages and watched both similarities and differences as our stories intertwined. With passion, Antoinette identifies purpose coupled with her skillful touch and precisely helps us face situations that we must overcome.

  Gracefully Broken helps us to navigate the roads of life while taking a different look at why we go through and how we can make it through tumultuous times. Her life becomes an open book of emotional, physical, and spiritual deficits which orders her steps and directs her path. As you dissect her life, you can understand your life better. Antoinette does for the reader the same thing she did for me over fifty-two years ago, helping us to see the sunshine, making a brighter day ahead regardless of insurmountable odds. Thanks, "my oldest friend in the world." You are surely God's masterpiece, a gift sent to the world to help us

GRACEFULLY BROKEN

to create beauty from the ashes that many of us are covered with.

Capatoria Z. Wilson

Senior Pastor
Healing Hearts International Ministries
Chicago, IL

FOREWORD
Apostle Regina Holliday

I met Antoinette while working as a nurse, in an extended care facility, over thirty years ago. We were co-workers who became friends and friends who became sisters. I have watched Antoinette go through many difficult situations and circumstances in her life but, I have also witnessed her triumphing through them. She has a heart for the broken and has always given her best when taking care of others in whatever capacity she operates in. Whether as a nurse, as a minister, as a sister, or as a friend, a spirit of excellence always compels her to go above and beyond. She does not just get the job done but she is determined to do the job well.

When she told me that she was writing a book, I intuitively knew that she was embarking on something that would not just bless her life but would bless the masses. As I read this book, I found myself getting a little emotional, at times, as I was reminded of the level of brokenness she has experienced. Other times, I became emotional because I could relate to some of the experiences she so transparently shares.

This book in your hands is your opportunity to sow generously into your own life. Reading this book and journeying through Antoinette's life, allows God to bring a harvest of revelation, healing and deliverance, on the seed you have so generously sown into yourself.

If you see yourself in any part of Antoinette's story, know that God wants to do the same for you as he has done for her. "Let God put the pieces together."

++Regina Holliday

Executive Pastor
Spreading The Word Worship Center
Chicago, IL.

DEDICATION

To Everyone: I would like to dedicate this book to a myriad of individuals. First, to every young person who feels where you are now is where you will always be. The conclusion of the whole matter to your story has yet to be written. As you navigate the terrain of life, know that many have traveled similar paths and come through with flying colors. What you did (pregnant as a teenager, committed a crime, attempted suicide, ran away from home, dropped out of school, or thought about giving up) is not who you are. God has a greater plan and a purpose for your life. To those who are being currently gracefully broken, let this book encourage you to know that with God ALL things are possible. Regardless of your age or stage in life, my prayer is that you will not allow the areas of brokenness to halt your destiny. Remember, God had a plan for your life before the foundation of the world.

GRACEFULLY BROKEN

To My Sons: Anthony, the heart of who you are remains intact regardless of the challenges faced. Traveling this journey with you evoked so many emotions. Feelings of grief and despair were turned to joy when I learned you were alive. Feelings of sadness loomed as I had to come to accept who you had now become. Also, feelings of love and joy to know that the core of who you are as a person, of genuine kindness, love, and having a natural sense of humor, holds me together on the daunting days. Thank you for allowing me to share a portion of your story.

To my youngest son, this book will be a constant reminder of your own talents. Like your mother, you have tenacity and drive to become all that God has called you to be. Thank you for the gift of my amazing grandson.

To My Family: Thank you for believing in me. Thank you for your consistent love and support.

GRACEFULLY BROKEN

To My Spiritual Leaders: Thank you Pastor Noah Nicholson II, for providing teaching, training, and correction to aid my development in the area of leadership and in ministry. Thank you to Archbishop William Hudson III and Pastor Andria Hudson for always stretching me beyond capacity to walk in the fullness of who God has ordained me to become. To Pastor Jarrett Perdue, thanks for a young man's wisdom and for always being available to dialogue about the right thing to do in challenging situations. To Apostle Jeffrey Holliday and Pastor Tori, thanks for birthing the spirit of intercession in my life. To Cecelia Mariner, Pastor Michael and Eleanor Williams thank you for teaching me what it means to commit to the call of God. To Addie McCafferty and Beverly Jones, thanks for the multiple confirming words that have propelled me to my destiny. I love you all. Lastly, to Apostle Regina Holliday, thank you for your guidance, your love, and your consistency in my life.

GRACEFULLY BROKEN

TABLE OF CONTENTS

Introduction - Why You? Why Now?............ 1

1 Broken in all the Right Places 10

2 The Root of Rejection 36

3 Parental Influence 51

4 Make Me Whole 69

5 The Pain Has Purpose 86

6 Mentorship Is Important 105

7 The Broken Mother 133

8 And We Know 160

INTRODUCTION
WHY YOU? WHY NOW?

In a world where many seek to put pen to paper through self-help books, leadership books, and training manuals, to help us become better, my first why is because He said so. Who is He? He is the Lord Jesus Christ. The journey to start this book has been tedious, tumultuous, and flooded with many tears and emotions. While I have received many words spoken over my life regarding me writing and publishing several books, I shuttered at the thought. How can this be? The cares of this world, fear, inadequacy, and so many other emotions, at the idea of sharing life lessons so painful and yet others so exhilarating, to arrive at the point of becoming gracefully broken.

In 2019, during a New Year's Eve Service, Bishop William Hudson III said to the congregation, but more specifically to me, "start the book, when you get home. Even if it is just a few words, start the book." This time, I obeyed the voice of the Lord and started writing the book and then I stopped. God sent several prophecies throughout that next year of 2020 to confirm His word. As one who is typically not a procrastinator, I realized "the time is now." I knew this when I received a random call from someone before I had awakened. She stated, "When are you going to finish the book?" (*Beverly Jones, your love, your support, and your encouragement are greatly appreciated*). I realized when I finally stopped resisting, and gave God a true yes, He allowed His grace to be readily available to assist me along this journey.

I recognized who I was then and who I am becoming are two different individuals? The process of becoming has been transformative, illuminating, and revelatory. Consequently, in the face of disappointments, tragedies, loss, rejection, and even fear, I have learned to adjust. Psychologists tell us that the first years of our lives are highly formative. What enters the mind, thought process, and emotions can either affect you negatively or positively. Our personal biases, coping skills, and preferences are readily established at an early age.

The imagery of broken that illuminates my mind is one of dropping a glass on the floor. The glass shatters into pieces so small whereby some parts are too difficult to see with the naked eye. Yet, when you walk barefoot on the floor where the brokenness occurred, you can get a piece of glass in the bottom of your foot that will make you jump to the sky. In some cases, our life is like shattered glass. We often miss the minute details. This prevents us from understanding how this miniature piece of glass has such a significant effect on the sum-total of who we are as people.

When the cut is left unattended, it can develop into a large wound. This wound can potentially become infected, requiring either antibiotics, or in some cases a debridement. Debridement, what on earth is that? Glad you asked. I failed to mention that I am a registered nurse by profession with over thirty years of healthcare experience. Debridement is a procedure for treating a wound in the skin. It is the removal of dead or damaged tissue to improve healthy tissue, creating an environment for healing to occur. Debridement every one-to-two weeks can increase the healing time to forty-two days.

This process can be painful (touch). The odor can provide a stench to your nostrils (smell). The assessment of the wound (sight) is critical for designing the treatment. The (sound) of a machine pulling out exudate is enough to make the average person cringe. The death of the cells occurs because of a lack of oxygen and interrupted blood flow. The healing process can take six to twelve weeks. In severe cases, debridement of a wound is performed with maggots. Left untreated, what started out as a small cut can potentially escalate to the area becoming gangrene. Gangrene usually affects the extremities and can result in the amputation of a limb. However, gangrene can also affect your internal organs. Gangrene is a medical emergency due to a lack of blood flow to tissues that could lead to death.

While there are natural consequences, there may also be spiritual ramifications. Consider taking your brokenness to the father. The Chief Physician requires free range to remove the damaged areas in your life. Allow Him to address the wound before the cells become necrotic (dead cells in your body/organ). Spiritually, suppose you fail to address small areas of brokenness. In that case, it can become a gaping wound that could lead to spiritual death.

My prayer to those reading this book is that God would blow His "pnuema", (Greek word meaning "breath" as something necessary for life) on every dead area in your life. Through the process of healing, may He address every malfunctioning cell that is slowly making essential areas in you inactive and move them to becoming active for His glory. Sometimes the hardest lessons are simple.

Navigate through your mind and meditate on how you allowed a minor offense (a small piece of broken glass in your foot) to go untreated. You were presented with many opportunities to forgive. Because you held on to the offense and did not address the "small piece of glass in your foot," now you have a necrotic wound and this will require weeks, months, and in some cases years to heal.

To promote healing, you must recognize the signs and symptoms. The signs are pain, swelling, numbness, and decreased sensation. Pain (loss of a loved one, death of a marriage or an estranged friendship). Swelling (tears have filled your eyes, the eyes are now swollen to the point of affecting your vision). Numbness in a specific body area (you have loss your ability to fight, but inwardly it is slowing manifesting outwardly). And finally, decreased sensation (you stop feeling anything in the area). However, I have some good news. Today is your day to receive deliverance to areas that have been masked. Today, we take the mask off and receive the debridement process to complete healing. The reason why is simple:

He Called Me To It!

GRACEFULLY BROKEN

GRACEFULLY BROKEN

CHAPTER 1
BROKEN IN ALL THE RIGHT PLACES

I have a confession to make. Before I take this deep dive into unchartered waters, please understand I have always been this person in the mind of God. Circumspectly, let us take a journey to explore the meaning of being broken and specific areas of brokenness in my life. It is time to take off the mask to uncover areas that have lied dormant. The little girl or boy on the inside can be healed from areas that broke them.

What does it mean to be *broken*? The definition of broken is, 'having been fractured or damaged and no longer in one piece or working order." The second definition is "having given up all hope; despairing. In Greek, the word broken is "suntribo" (soon-tree-bo), which means to be battered, crushed, mauled, or broken into pieces. As you navigate this book, take a moment to reflect on any area you have experienced brokenness. Ask God, as you read this book to uncover hidden places and heal you from the inside out.

Brokenness can include any of the following: the death of a child or parent, a divorce, feeling of hopelessness (as if life will not get any better), loss of a career, being overlooked for a promotion, social isolation, or rejection. I come to encourage you and let you know; God is ready to put the pieces together again. When I think of glass shattered on the floor, I realize that some of the pieces were not designed to be put back together. In life, every broken relationship was not for the purpose of being put back together. The pain experienced had a purpose. The purpose could be to develop you naturally, spiritually, emotionally, financially, and psychologically. My desire is to encourage you not to succumb to what broke you. Instead, allow the process to promote growth.

Finances is an area in which I experienced brokenness. It can be challenging to manage financial brokenness when you were never given the tools to learn about budgeting, saving, and even stewardship over those things in your possession. While a viable option, filing bankruptcy could have been prevented if I had been taught how to budget my finances.

One memory of my childhood that stands out is my mother's ability to keep a roof over our heads, clothes on our backs, and feed us, with enough left to give to those in need. When I look back, I recognize she budgeted in such a manner, that we never knew how much we did not have. However, the wisdom of her ability to manage money was taught when my siblings and I worked a summer job. We were required to purchase our school clothes for the upcoming year and contribute a small (it seemed enormous then) dollar amount to the household. She taught my siblings and me how to buy personal items and shop on a budget. It amazes me that when we become adults, we start to freelance and forget the basic principles taught during our childhood and adolescent years. The level of leadership demonstrated by my mother was not without notice in my adult life. She could have allowed us to spend our money frivolously. Yet, she taught responsibility and stewardship to teenagers.

Let's say, you are one of those individuals who has filed bankruptcy in the past. Your experience taught you how to handle your finances. While growing in this area, a pandemic occurs, and one spouse loses a job with no prospects in sight. Immediately, the memories of the past will illuminate your thought process and you can find yourself feeling sad or discouraged.

The experience of poverty or lack can break many. The worst feeling in the world for a parent is not being able to provide. It is not about private schools, designer clothes or the latest updated cell phones. The poverty and lack I am describing is when you do not have enough food to eat and you must figure out how to feed a family of five, when you only have enough for three. This reminds me of a time when as a single mother, my gas hand was on E, and I did not have enough gas to make it to a gas station, let alone gas to make it to work. People faced with such dilemmas can move from feelings of hurt to feelings of shame. The shame moves to embarrassment and leads to pride. I have heard statements like, "I do not want anyone to know my business." In my personal experience, I felt the shame of having to always call my dad when I had more month than money. My granny used to say, "Closed mouths don't get fed." We should not be made to feel that we are less of a parent when we fall on hard times. Secondly, we should not be afraid to ask for help.

Every experience of brokenness you encounter has purpose, whether you can see it or not. What purpose would God have in allowing you and your children to go hungry, get evicted, or experience a job loss because of a lack of resources? Did the situation come from God? The process can push us to a level of creativity we have yet to explore. Have you ever found yourself in a situation and you told yourself, "I will not make this mistake again?" A true lesson learned will teach you how to stretch food, budget money, and purchase what is needed than rather what you want. While I have no issues with nice things, it is important to live within our means.

We must learn the difference between a want and a need. Every sacrifice you make comes with a cost. To obtain a higher education is a sacrifice. This sacrifice might cause you to miss out on valuable time with your children, family or friends and will cost you financially. Do you choose to make the sacrifice now, to provide a better future for them later? If you make this choice, even though it is a positive choice, you may find out later how this choice affected those around you.

Children want and need the presence of their parents. When a parent chooses to pursue a higher education for a better paying job, the child might feel the parent was not there for them. Each child needs a parent in a different way. When we make a decision, we make it knowing that everyone that will be affected by it will not be pleased. How often have you heard of a woman pursuing higher education and the husband leaves because he thinks she does not need him anymore. Most women would rather have their marriage intact. On those rare occasions, you might run across someone who is career-driven and pursue their version of success at the cost of a relationship or children. We should not hold them hostage and condemn their decision. Providing support to a spouse, a family member, or a loved one could divert the impact of potential brokenness by using the simple element called communication. Broken children can become broken parents. Unless the cycle is reversed, it will continue to repeat itself.

Money is not the root of all evil, but the love of money is. Money is not the answer to some of our problems. Where are you? You may be thinking, "How did I get here? I am not supposed to be here?" Deborah Cox penned the words to the song "Nobody's Supposed to Be Here." How did you get to the place of brokenness in your finances? Discipline and knowledge are what we need most. Also, it takes knowledge to understand how to make a budget. If this is an area you have been broken in, consider taking a course or a webinar on how to formulate a budget.

If you know emphatically that God has positioned you for wealth, you do not want to wait until it shows up to learn how to manage the resources. Your multi-million-dollar plan should already be on paper. The bible declares in Habakkuk 2:2, *"Write the vision and make it plain."* If you lack vision for your resources, be a good steward over what you have, and God will provide the increase. To be a good steward, means giving God what you owe Him first.

We have a responsibility to protect that which God has entrusted to us. As good stewards, we preserve our peace, our joy, our family, our finances, our careers, our faith, and the word of God. Our wealth is more significant than our bank accounts. The scripture declares in Psalm 112:3 (NASB), *"Wealth and riches are in the house of the righteous, and his righteousness endures forever.*
Everything we have belongs to God. He entrusts some things to us to steward over and we want to be found not hiding them under a bushel but multiplying them to the glory of God our Father.

Malachi 3:10 (KJV) says, *"Bring ye all the tithes into the storehouse, that there may be meat in mine house, and prove me now herewith, saith the Lord of hosts, if I will not open you the windows of heaven, and pour out a blessing, that there shall not be room enough to receive.*

Prayer: Father in the name of Jesus, teach us how to be a good steward of those things you have entrusted unto us. Many of us have never been taught how to handle money. We understand everything we have belongs to you. Teach us your ways and we will endeavor to put you first in the area of our finances and every area of our life. In Jesus Name. Amen!

How many areas of your life have you experienced brokenness? For me personally, divorce was an area that attributed to another area of brokenness in my life. Marriage counseling and self-development could have prevented me from giving my ex-husband a YES, when God intended for me to "just say no." Yes, I get it, my ex-husband was fine as wine in the summertime. He checked some of the boxes that I had designed. However, when he exhibited specific attributes, I overlooked them thinking, I could change someone who had already become the core of who they would become. When we allow our emotions to drive our decision-making process, things may not turn out as we envisioned. Instead, we look for someone other than ourselves to blame.

    When I met my ex-husband, I was what most would consider a babe in Christ. He "found me," while I was administering immunizations in a public housing project called Hilliard Homes in Chicago, Illinois. He pursued me feverously. One day, he said, "I want to take you on a 'Pretty Woman' shopping spree." Most who know me are aware this is one of my favorite movies. He did not know this was the case, but the enemy (inner me) did. During the shopping spree, we walked into a jewelry store. He purchased a ring and proposed on one knee in the store. When I reflect on the event, it was something like in a movie. The staff in the store were clapping, on-lookers in the mall were cheering, and I was standing there not sure of what to say. At this point in the relationship, I was not in love with him. I loved the idea of him. I marveled at the thought "It's my turn." My friends were now married, and I said to myself, "Well, he did find me."

The bible declares in Proverbs 18:22, *"whoso findeth a wife findeth a good thing, and obtaineth favor of the Lord."* As a babe in Christ, I analyzed the situation and circumstances and concluded the following: you did not go looking for him, he found you. He pursued you. You did not pursue him. He asked to come to church with you. He was a believer in Jesus Christ. With limited understanding of the scripture, this seemed like the next step. What you did not hear me say is "I love him so much." Again, I loved the idea of him, getting married, having a wedding, receiving assistance in raising my sons, working together financially, and legal sex. *Let that sink in.*

During our marriage counseling session, Pastor Mosley said to him, "what if I said no to you marrying her?" He replied, "Well, I would just take her somewhere else and marry her." I believed he was serious. You did hear me say he was serious. You see, there was something in my gut that I was not sure about. However, at this time, the invitations are being printed. Everyone is aware of the engagement, and my two other friends who believed God for a husband were married. Now, it was my turn. If I can encourage anyone with this story, my first and last words will be to make sure you know the voice of the Lord. The scripture says in John 10:27-28 (KJV), *"My sheep hear my voice, and I know them, and they follow me."* If I had known His voice, I would have called the wedding off two weeks before the ceremony. I take full responsibility for messing up his life. Why do you say that? I did not know who I was in God when I married my ex-husband. He was not the issue. We were just unequally yoked, and I did not understand what that entailed.

He had a relationship with God, yet our lives were headed in different directions. His views on what he expected from his wife were different from my ideas. I remember he came home from work one day, and I was listening to a preaching tape by Bishop T. D. Jakes. He said out loud, "this chick loves T. D. Jakes more than she loves me." The reality is when we married, I had just started to fall in love with the word of God and with God. He did not sign up for being married to someone who was being birthed into ministry. Also, in the words of my former pastor, Bishop Nicholson, he was sent as my assignment to draw him closer to Christ, but instead, I married the assignment. I believe God intended for me to be the vessel to draw him closer to what God called him to do, instead I viewed him as an answer to a prayer.

Most would admit they have a "certain type" in their imagination or thoughts. In full transparency, I recall refusing to give one individual the time of day, solely because he was "not my type." I remember vividly hearing in my spirit, "your type is not working for you." What a revelation? Our type can limit us and lead us to emotional brokenness that could take years to be delivered from. What do you mean by having a type? As a woman, do you want him to have a specific credit score, possess a certain height, weight, and body build? Does the thought of him having children or not wanting children disqualify him from the list? Will his educational degree make the list or better than that, will you limit him to a specific race, creed, or color? If so, you have a type.

Please listen attentively. There is absolutely nothing wrong with having a standard. However, do not limit God to your list, but instead trust Him to know who you need and what you need as well. Marriage is a covenant designed by God to reflect his relationship with the church. He is the bridegroom, and we are His bride. This analogy demonstrates how important we are to Him. Our standard should be based on the word of God. Yet, if you are unlearned in the scriptures, as I was, you might acquiesce to taking matters into your own hands to speed up the process. The bible records several instances when women and men such as Abram, Sarai, Rachel, and Leah took matters into their own hands. My decision-making process was focused on the physical and not the spiritual, which allowed me to be a major contributing factor in the broken process.

Hiding the truth of your pain from others and not admitting it to yourself will leave you in a state of brokenness. I could not even share the pain of being divorced after a short stint of marriage with my best friend. You see, two of my friends and I had prayed and agreed in prayer regarding God blessing us with a husband. The two friends remain married twenty-five years later. Initially, the pain from the brokenness caused me to not want to be around them. Hanging out with them was a reminder of a failed marriage. How did I miss the mark? Did I not hear God clearly? As I sought to continue to develop my relationship with the father, I realized that God is omniscient. Omniscient means, "He knows everything."

My failed marriage was not a surprise to God. My choice to marry the joker was not a surprise to God. Rest in this today; HE KNEW! He knows right where you are today. Pastor Nicholson would make this statement often, and each time it irritated me to no end. He stated, "You are where you are because of the choices you have made." I find it interesting to know, with all confidence, that the Lord knew exactly what right choice I would make and what wrong choice I would make.

Do you recall the conversation about the steps needed to heal a wound? If you skip a step in the natural process of wound healing, you could find yourself having to start over. Now the healing times are multiplied. Most people are not self-aware; they have not been conditioned to take self-inventory. Instead, they would rather place the blame for their dysfunction on someone other than themselves. They walk away feeling rejected and waiting for another man to validate their worth. I had to learn what God said in His word concerning marriage. One of the best treatments for me was to cancel the pity party and take inventory of myself. I married him not knowing who I was in God. I allowed him to choose me when I did not know myself. You see, my situation is not unique. When we are no longer faced with an area of brokenness, we take for granted that the site is no longer an issue. While you may have suppressed it, it can show up in other areas of your life.

While the divorce papers were signed, the shame of the divorce flooded my thoughts. The feelings associated with the dissolution of the marriage left me broken. I was forced to ask myself some tough questions. Did I miss something? This is when I decided to study what God said about marriage. I did not want to repeat this mistake.

There is no shame in desiring a husband. The problem comes when your desire becomes so intense that it attracts what you like and not what God has in His plan for your life. Dismiss the misnomer that there are no "good men" left on the earth. If God made you a promise, rest assured, He will keep it. He is the ultimate promise keeper. Take time in your single state and get to know your authentic self.

If you are reading this book and struggling with choices you have made that might not have been the right choice, please forgive yourself. When I learned how to hear the voice of God, He shared something with me that was life-changing and life-giving. He said, "I gave you what you wanted, and not what I had for you." Let us not focus so much on marriage as the end-all to our lives that we get what we want and not what He wants for us. I am preaching better than y'all saying AMEN!

Most, not all, have experienced heartbreak from relationships. The one we loved was supposed to love us back. The one we stood at the altar and made a covenant with was supposed to last until death do us part. Yet, the relationship ended and left you feeling broken. The person you believed was "the one" was not someone you would spend the rest of your life with. The most heartbreaking experience for me was allowing someone to choose me when I did not know who I was. I could never be mad at or hold a grudge against my ex-husband. He met me at a time when I had just started to develop my relationship with God. He was not prepared for his new wife loving someone else. When we do not know who we are, we can allow ourselves to be chosen by someone who should be a part of our history and not our destiny.

Relationships can take us back in our mind to previous experiences. We can fail to see the connection as to why we "keep choosing the same people." Earlier, I discussed having "a type." Suppose you find yourself repeatedly involved with someone who is physically or verbally abusive. In that case, it is time to assess the root of the choice. I do not want you to miss the vital component because you must do a root cause analysis to discover how the foundation was laid. Could it be you saw someone abuse your mother or your father? Yes, men can and do experience abuse. Did you come from a family where everyone got divorced and no one was able to sustain a successful relationship? If you are sexually promiscuous at a young age, stop to consider if your environment played a factor in your decision-making process. Sometimes, when a person is abused, they can potentially become the abuser. The situations may not necessarily be a reflection of their own choices. Instead, some circumstances have more to do with the choice of others and not ourselves. Once you find out the who, what, when, and how, you can heal from areas that broke you and formulated your choices. Please do not allow blame and shame to prevent you from moving from broken to being made whole.

As a single mother, I was described as dominant. The reality is the men I allowed to choose me did not assume the role and responsibility as the father. I found myself placed in a role that I was not designed nor created for. Women raising children as a single mother bear the weight of navigating through two roles. I was never the replacement for their father. No one will ever take the place of a father. The reality is some women are not dominant and robust by choice. Men who do not assume their God-given place to be the priest, protector, and family provider have left the women without a will. What happened to the women who could bring home the bacon, fry it up in the pan and never let him forget he is a man? Men, we really do not want to compete, only to compliment.

Broken in all the right places positions us to see the grace of God in our lives. Whether you have gone through a divorce, had a child out of wedlock, or have never had the privilege of knowing the identity of your biological parent, there is a balm in Gilead. This a balm that provides healing for every broken area in your life. Allow the Lord to put the pieces together.

Prayer: *Father, in the name of Jesus, we come today and ask for you to heal your children from any area in their lives that has resulted in brokenness. Lord, make them whole. Thank you, Father, for "nothing missing, and nothing broken" in the lives of your children. You told us in your word that everything that concerns us, concerns you. Heal your people today, In Jesus Name, We Pray! Amen!*

_____

_____

_____

_____

_____

GRACEFULLY BROKEN

GRACEFULLY BROKEN

GRACEFULLY BROKEN

CHAPTER 2
THE ROOT OF REJECTION

There is not a situation in your life, where you cannot find help in the scriptures. Our brokenness is not unique. While none of us raised our hands and volunteered for the assignment to be broken, we understand there is healing and deliverance available to us through the word of God. Truthfully, some areas of brokenness go back to our ancestors. Individuals throughout biblical times, experienced some of the same issues you and I face today. Issues that were not confronted by our ancestors, lost the capacity to be conquered in their space of time. We cannot conquer what we are not willing to confront. We must first have knowledge of the issue to possess the capacity to confront it. The family secrets of rejection, sexual abuse, poverty, criminal histories, or discovering the person you thought was your parent is not your parent. Television shows that provide DNA results to determine paternity are stressful as you wait to hear "you are not the father." This news can be earth-shattering. As the crowd cheers, laughs and make snide remarks, the parents are experiencing devastation or in some cases relief. Paternity is not a new subject. The pain of unidentified paternity could be a vehicle to allow the entrance for the spirit of rejection.

In the bible, there is a story of two sisters by the name of Leah and Rachel. This story depicts rejection in a relationship. Rachel is described as a beautiful woman. When Jacob shared his first kiss with her, he lifted his voice and wept. Jacob asked her father Laban, for her hand in marriage. He willingly worked for seven years to receive her as his wife. However, her father Laban tricked Jacob. After he worked seven years, instead of accepting his bride Rachel, he was presented with Leah.

Leah is described as tender eyed or in modern-day vernacular, "cross-eyed." Leah was the first woman in a second position. If that does not reek of rejection, then I do not know what does. Imagine being given to be espoused to a man who did not want you. You see, Leah was the oldest daughter and should have been given to marriage first. Genesis 29:31 (KJV) says, *"When the Lord saw that Leah was hated, he opened her womb: but Rachel was barren."* Leah started producing baby after baby in hopes that her husband would love her. Does this sound at all familiar? Why are we envious of others and what they possess when what they have did not originate from them? While Rachel had the physical beauty and love of her husband, she could not produce a child. Leah did not open her own womb; God did. Rachel was envious that her sister was producing children and she was not. Often, we look on the outside of a situation without the complete information and judge based on appearance. We want what others have based on appearance, without considering what it cost them to receive the promise.

Today, bareness can take on a different connotation because some women have no desire to have a child. Yet, in biblical times, barrenness was frowned upon. Leah had to feel a tremendous amount of rejection. Leah kept producing children hoping her husband would love her, like some women today. In my sanctified imagination, I can see the root of her rejection starting with her father. Could it be that even her father was not sure if a man would, of his own free-will, select Leah as his bride? When God saw that she was unloved, he opened her womb and Rachel remained unable to produce a child. Leah might not have been the finest woman in the room, but she had favor with God. Leah's father said to Jacob, *"fulfill her week, and we will give thee also for the service which thou shalt serve with me yet another seven years."* Translation: Enjoy the honeymoon with her for one week, and then I will give you Rachel. But it will cost you another seven years of work. There is another adjective for what her father did. SELAH!

    Now enters phase two of the rejection. Rachel looks at her sister producing baby after baby, and she is barren.

Now the tables of rejection have turned. It does not matter your physical beauty (attributed to Rachel) or your inner strength (attributed to Leah) at some point, we all have experienced some form of rejection. The question on the table is, "what will be your response to the rejection? Leah focused on what she was able to produce. Genesis 29:35 (NIV) records: *She conceived again, and when she gave birth to a son, she said "This time I will praise the Lord. So she named him Judah. Then she stopped having children.* Leah decided to glorify the father and not focus her attention on waiting to be accepted by her husband. Rachel was not producing and envied her sister.

The bible declares in Genesis 30:1, *"When Rachel saw that she was not bearing Jacob any children, she became jealous of her. So she said to Jacob (her husband), "Give me children, or I'll die."* That is a strong statement. The sister's rejection put them in a posture of competition. They started utilizing their handmaids to bore children. The sisters took matters into their own hands. The rejection spirit did not stop with the sisters but then trickled down to the children. Herein lies generational curses. The small cut lingered before aid was rendered. The wound grew into a gangrenous situation that lacked oxygen to the tissues, resulting in broken relationships between Laban and Jacob and the sisters.

Those navigating through this journey can attest to experiencing some level of rejection. Whether it occurred in the home when one child seemed to be favored more than the other, not being picked for the basketball or cheerleading team, or even feeling as if you were treated like the "black sheep" of the family. If rejection is not carefully dealt with, it can cause you to reject yourself. If carefully traced, it can stem from our formative years. Rejection starts as a seed planted in our lives through various life experiences. When you imagine a tree, you know the foundation of the tree is in the roots. If the roots are damaged, the fruit the tree produces will also be damaged.

We are like our spiritual parents Adam and Eve. They could eat freely of every tree in the garden, except the tree of good and evil. We always seem to want what we cannot have. The tree of rejection has deep roots. We need to make a choice to not only eat from the right tree but decide to do the work necessary to dig up the roots and pluck it out. Plucking out the roots, can prevent the production of rotten fruit for future generations.

We have all experienced word curses spoken over our life. I must share the importance of not allowing the words spoken by others to break you. Sometimes these comments come from those we respect, admire, or those that should love us. When a teacher tells a student, "you will never be anything," the words could open the door for another level of brokenness. Spiritual leaders are responsible for watching over your soul. Negative words spoken over your life by the leader can leave lasting impressions that could derail your destiny. I personally was affected by negative words spoken directly to me when I sought counseling when my marriage was in trouble. My pastor who had married us had died. We scheduled an appointment at the new church we attended. As an organized person, I decided to write a note on issues that needed to be addressed. I did not want to get emotional and not focus on the real problems. To my surprise, or shall I say, "shock and awe," she started the session by saying, "you talk too much." I did not hear anything else she said in the session because immediately, I went back to the second-grade report card where I received the comments TALKS! TALKS! TALKS!

    Often people are not aware of where you come from or previous assaults you have experienced. I am sure the pastor had no idea that her words would send me back into a cave that closed my mouth when I should have been free to express myself. One of the reasons for this transparency is to set someone free. I saw this same pastor many years later and at that time, my foundation was stronger. I was able to speak to her and hold a friendly conversation because the brokenness of those words spoken twice in my life had been healed. These situations had to occur so that when I began to open my mouth and proclaim the gospel, I could do it with the assurance of who was backing up my words. Romans 8:28 says, *"And we know that all things work together for good to them that love God, to them that are called according to His purpose."* Instead of allowing the rejection to take root, I learned to let the negative words drive me to my purpose. Stop allowing what they said to you to stop you from, not just being broken, but even allowing you the freedom to be made whole.

    Rejection enters our lives when we have no understanding of what it means and how it can affect us. Unfortunately, we tend to see people as we are. Maybe, you grew up in a home with bitterness, hatred, ill-spoken and profane words as the formative language or even the lack of receiving affection. The result of these characteristics took root and shaped who you became as an adult. Most, if not all of us, have experienced some form of rejection. The rejection can stifle you and hinder you from moving forward if you are not aware of its existence. The good news is the bible declares Jesus was rejected and despised among men. Even though He who knew no sin, went through rejection, He came out on the other side victorious, because the rejection was a part of His purpose.

It is imperative to chew the meat and spit out the bones. When negative words are spoken, we must examine if there is any truth in what is being said. If there is no foundational truth, we reject the words that are attempting to plant a seed of rejection in our lives. For example, if someone tells you, "No one will ever love you." That is not true. The bible declares in Romans 5:7-9,

"For scarcely for a righteous man will one die: yet peradventure for a good man some would even dare to die. But God commendeth his love toward us while we were yet sinners, Christ died for us". Yes, someone already loves you. And His name is Jesus. He is waiting for you to exchange the root of rejection for an everlasting love. Love is an action word. John 3:16 (KJV) says, *For God so loved the world that he gave his only begotten Son, that whosoever believeth in him should not perish, but have everlasting life.* Today, examine the root of the rejection, go to the Lord, and ask Him to heal your heart. He is waiting for you.

Psalm 147:3 *says, He healeth the broken heart and bindeth up their wounds.*

Prayer: *In the name of Jesus, Father I come today and stand in the gap for those who are struggling after the brokenness of divorce or with the spirit of rejection. Lord, I pray that you heal every area of brokenness in their lives.*

GRACEFULLY BROKEN

Lord, you are the mender of the broken-hearted. Lord, please heal their hearts today. Remind them that you are nigh unto the broken-hearted. Lord, allow them to draw closer to you. Show them who they are in you. You said in your word, they are the apple of your eye. Remind them, that they are fearfully and wonderfully made. Their price is far above rubies. Just as the veil in the temple was torn from top to bottom, remind them that your love for them is so exceptional that it will tear up anything separating us from you. To those waiting for a God-ordained relationship, renew their strength. Lord, strengthen their resolve. Give them a nevertheless attitude. You know what is best for your children. You have declared their ending from the beginning. You know the plans you have for them, thoughts of peace and not evil, to get them to an expected end. Lord, help those that may be stuck in a cycle of repeating the same mistakes. Give them the heart to accept your forgiveness and help them to forgive themselves. Let them hear you speak in their spirit that they are not a failure, that you love them with an everlasting love. Lord, I thank you that those who have even fallen into an adulterous or fornicating lifestyle because of loneliness and emptiness, that you are drawing them back to you. Remind your children, the void can only be filled by your presence. Lord, you said in your word, he that hunger and thirst after righteousness shall be filled. Fill them with your love, fill them with your presence. Let them know you have accepted them into the family of the beloved. In Jesus Name, I pray, AMEN!

GRACEFULLY BROKEN

GRACEFULLY BROKEN

CHAPTER 3
PARENTAL INFLUENCE

As a young girl, I demonstrated the capacity to possess leadership skills. My mother confirmed that I was independent and did not require as much direction as my other siblings. As I look back over my life, there were specific junctures where I really could have used additional directives from my mother. The recall of a kitchen table experience was one of the pivotal points in my development. I have so many instances in my childhood that seems to be a blur. The incident I am about to describe remains formidable and helps me understand what I could not comprehend at the young age of seven. I now invite you to meet my parental influences and share a kitchen table experience.

Our parents have a significant impact on shaping our lives. Whether you were raised by an abusive mother or a loving mother, the seeds that are sown into your life affect your development. My mother loved to read books and newspapers. She prepared breakfast every morning before school, and you could rest assured that at five in the evening, we sat for dinner as a family. My mother was not the most outwardly affectionate person. However, she demonstrated her love for her children with her actions. My mother is supportive, direct, and possess strong leadership capacities. At the time, she was active in our community and well respected. My mother has always been one who does not mince words or sugar coat truth. If you wanted an honest answer, you could ask her. If you wanted her to tell you what you wanted to hear, then do not ask her.

My mother believed in getting an education. As parents, we should want our children to go farther than we could ever imagine. My mother did not miss a parent-teacher's conference. In grade school, parents met with teachers face to face to discuss the child's progress. Instead of taking us with her, she would return and hold a round table discussion to review our progress report cards after meeting with the teachers. Now we enter the kitchen table experience. While my three siblings and I sat at the table, I anxiously awaiting to hear the teachers comments on my progress. When my turn for feedback came, she acknowledged that I had earned all E's and G's. The letter grade E stood for excellent and G stood for good. I sat smiling and with a proud look on my face (God hates this). My mother then proceeded to read the back of the progress report card. The comment by the teacher read in capital letters, "TALKS, TALKS, and TALKS." This is the avenue where the seed was planted that caused the trigger in my marriage counseling as previously mentioned. My siblings and I laughed. My mother is a serious person, with whom I share some of those attributes. She did not play when it came to behaving in school or anywhere else for that matter. She stated, "You think that's funny. I do not send you to school to just run your mouth." She looked at me in a manner that made me feel like she would give me a whipping but thank God she did not. She put the fear of God in me. I did not repeat that mistake again. Well, at least while I lived with her. This would have been an excellent place to insert the phrase "Mom, what had happened was??"

As a second grader, with no foundation in God, I had no insight, hindsight, or foresight that the Lord would call me to preach the gospel. The concept was not even an afterthought. Yes, He could have revealed His will in the formative years of my life. My road to brokenness took a different trajectory. Jesus tells us that unless we become as little children, we will not inherit the kingdom of God. I am returning to my roots to show you how at a young age, without being brought up in a Christian home, the hand of the Lord was on me to use my words to heal the brokenhearted. Luke 4:18 (KJV) says it like this: "*The spirit of the Lord is upon me because (there is a reason) He has anointed me to preach the gospel to the poor, he hath sent me (I did not just go, He sent me) to heal the brokenhearted, to preach deliverance to the captives, and recovering of sight to the blind, to set at liberty them that are bruised.*

Although my parents were no longer together, my father remained active in my life. I recall a time once when my dad visited one day. During the visit, he stated, "Do not sit on any man's lap and do not call anyone daddy except me?" Every time I think of this statement as an adult, I laugh within myself. I asked him this question a few years ago as an adult, "Did that statement only apply as a child?" You will get that later or next week. Ultimately, even though he was no longer in the home, he was marking his territory. The statement or declaration was one to establish who he was in my life. Little did I know that the lack of his presence in my physical home would open a door for my brokenness? The spirit of rejection entered and attempted to take a firm root in my life. Keep in mind, I had no understanding of the nature of rejection at the time. His physical absence affected me in ways I had yet to discover. At this point, the spirit of rejection entered to attempt to deliver a strong root in my life. BUT GOD!

My dad married and had two additional children. He would promise to pick my sister and I up on the weekend and bring us to his house or for summer visits. Often, I would sit in the window watching the cars drive by anxiously awaiting his arrival. When a car drove pass, my eyes would light up, and I would say, "Here he comes!" Unfortunately, he failed to show up on multiple occasions. I am not sure if he called my mother to let her know he would not make it. All I understood at this age and stage of my life was that he had another family. I felt unimportant, as if I no longer mattered. It still amazes me to see how the enemy will induce the spirit of rejection at a young age before you ever find out who you were created to become. I have and will forever be a daddy's girl and that is no shade on my mother.

My mother has always been the glue to hold the family together. So, why would I place more emphasis on my father than my mother? As I look back over my life, I, like so many other children, wanted the experience of a two-parent home without understanding the variables associated with adult relationships. My parents tell a tale of two cities, yet the accounts had nothing to do with my parents not loving or caring for me. The truth of the matter is my mother had every right to feel a sense of rejection from me when I would run away to my father's house. I am sure she thought within herself, (*paraphrased*) "This little girl got a lot of nerve running away to her father. I am the one making sure she is fed, clothed, and taught fundamental principles of integrity, compassion, and a work ethic."

The absence of my father allowed the entrance of the spirit of rejection. At the age of seven, you cannot understand why a relationship did not work. Rejection is defined as releasing or letting go of something or someone. It involves treating something or someone in a way that makes them feel devalued. Today, I can honestly attest that this was a trick of the enemy. My father demonstrated love and respect when we were together. Yet, in his physical absence, the gait was opened for the spirit of rejection to creep in. By the age of thirteen, I found myself running away from home every Friday. I would take the bus and the train to my father's house. Was it just to be with him? Was it to experience the love and adoration of a father? Honestly, I do not know.

As a little girl, I vividly remember my dad taking my sister and me to dinner and a movie. We ate at a fancy restaurant in downtown Chicago after watching the movie "Lady Sings the Blues." I am not sure why he took us to this movie at our age, but the interaction was more important than the movie title. My dad loves to sing and considers himself to be good at harmonizing. As we ate dinner, he sang the song "Someday We Will Be Together." The experience we shared was life changing. The hole in my rejected heart was plugged up. This is the moment when I started to move from being broken to being healed, so I thought.

When destiny and purpose are on your life, and the enemy is denied access to a specific door, he seeks another entry point. While now having a bandage applied to the wound, nothing prepared me for the wound to open again.

In my senior year of high school, I became pregnant with my first child. When I called my dad to tell him I was pregnant, he stated, "So what are you going to do now? Are you just going to drop out of school, get on public aid, and keep having babies?" Wow!!! What a statement for an already broken teenager to hear. I replied, No, and hung up the phone. Rejection by my father, in addition to the stares and whispers of others, once the pregnancy was evident, was a lot for a teenage girl to take.

This small cut started to turn into a big hole of rejection and opened another door for the spirit of abandonment. How could my dad abandon me at such an important point in my life? Did he even realize the impact of the words he spoke over my life? I recall riding the State Street bus in Chicago. On the bus was a sign that read, "Words hit as hard as a fist." I will never forget the truthfulness of this statement. I realized my dad had no idea of the wound he placed in my heart that contributed to the processing of my brokenness. I was too young to even understand his life, let alone his life experiences. We tend to look for blame. The reality is, the rejection and abandonment were developed on a foundation long before I ever came on the scene.

My paternal grandfather was in and out of my paternal grandmother's life. My father told me stories of how hurt his mother was with the inconsistencies of my grandfather in the lives of him and his siblings. My grandmother always "took him back" per my dad. Could it be my dad (without knowledge) was protecting his heart, or mirroring behaviors he learned? I never considered the fact that he could have been hurt, disappointed, or concerned about what would become of my life as a young mother. The only thing that was sure, was that I felt like he abandoned me at one of the most critical junctures of my life.

My mother's reaction was different. One day after coming home from working a summer job, I talked to her about buying a ten-speed bike when I got paid. She quietly replied, "I don't think that's a good idea since you are pregnant. I made you an appointment for August 26, at

9am, to see the doctor." In comparison to my dad, her reaction was priceless. I sat at the foot of her bed astounded. As I prepared to graduate high-school, I realized I was still affected by my father's response. When I graduated from high school, I told my mother I would not give my dad a ticket to my graduation. Obviously, I was still hurt. Yet, the wisdom of my mother spoke and simply stated, "Yes, you are."

My mother played such a significant role in providing balance by allowing me to be a teenager and setting limits. Even though I was seventeen, I was still a mother with responsibilities. Becoming a mother, opened yet another door for rejection. People have a way of looking at you differently when you become pregnant as a teenager and you are not married. Without my mother's help and her wisdom, I am not sure how I would have made it. She held me accountable for my son's life. The foundation of a work ethic, integrity, and responsibility was laid and formulated in my DNA.

At times, she would allow me to participate in my favorite hobby of skating. Other times, she would not allow me to go and allowed me to feel the weight of being a teenage mother. Becoming a parent is not without its own challenges. Single parenting was even more challenging. My mother never made me feel condemned. Instead, she provided grace. Grace is the free and unmerited favor of God. God does not always give us what we rightfully deserve. Basically, my mom gave me what I did not deserve. As my mother, she could have quickly rejected me, put me out of the house, sent me to live with my dad, or just left me to the streets. Instead, she moved in silence and was making preparation without my knowledge. Well, this is just like God.

Today, some of you might still be experiencing the rejection from words spoken over your life that were damaging. The individuals who spoke the words could have spoken them out of anger, frustration, or disappointment. Also, alcohol, drugs, generational curses, or even ignorance of not knowing the effect could have been contributing factors. You do not want to allow others, regardless of the rationale, to abort the destiny God has for your life. If you were told like I was, "you talk too much," when the time comes for you to open your mouth to defend a dissertation for a doctorate degree, sing for the opera, preach to nations, or pray for a friend, the ghost of words past could stop you dead in your tracks. You must forgive the offence and the offender. Do not allow the words to rent a space in your head and paralyze you from moving forward.

Most parents can see the potential in their children before they see it within themselves. When a child's life looks contrary to their God-given potential, parents might experience a sense of guilt as if they did not do enough to help them navigate the path. While other parents recognize, that some mistakes their children make is based on their choices and not an indictment against the parent. If the mother tells the child, "Do not touch the iron, it's hot." The curiosity of the child leads to touching the iron and getting burned. The lesson the child learned was not through the instruction of the parent but through the experience.

Our parents did the best they knew how with the capacity they possessed. The decisions made or words spoken could have been what was mirrored in their environment. It does not make sense to hold hatred, animosity, or even personal pain in your heart toward the present or absent parent. God wants you to be whole. If your life is fragmented with many small intricate broken pieces, let me remind you, "He can put pieces together." Some pieces that have broken do not need to be a part of the reconstruction but remain an indelible memory to prevent stepping on that piece of broken glass again.

Prayer: *Father, in the name of Jesus, we ask that you heal us from every parental influence that knowingly or unknowingly opened the door to rejection. Father, heal us from the generational curses that allowed the spirit of depression, alcoholism, drug addiction and/or mental illness, to enter illegally. Lord, we go back seven generations and cancel the assignment of the enemy that opened the door in the lives of our families to leave us broken. We decree and declare the curse is broken and will not be passed down any further in our bloodline. Lord, restore the parental relationships. You said in your word, healing is the children's bread. Heal today, in Jesus name.*

_____

_____

_____

_____

_____

_____

GRACEFULLY BROKEN

GRACEFULLY BROKEN

CHAPTER 4
MAKE ME WHOLE

The definition of the word whole means "all of; entire and in an unbroken or undamaged state; in one piece. The objective is to be in an unbroken or undamaged state of mind. When we allow words spoken or deeds done in the flesh to break us, (because we are human), we must first recognize the areas that are damaged or broken and seek repair. Yes, I know he told you he loved you and would be with you forever, but he would not stop hitting you. I know she told you she would seek help, but every time she got drunk, she cursed you out again. Verbal, emotional, sexual, and mental abuse, regardless of the perpetrator is still abuse. In my opinion, treatments of cruelty by someone saying they love you is one of the worst forms of abuse. If you allow yourself to sweep the issue under the rug and not address it, you will discover it manifests in several other forms.

There are many areas of damaged areas in our lives. Overeating, not eating, eating and throwing up immediately after, depression, aggression, and even regression will show up. In the African American community, seeking professional help is taboo. Individuals that have been labeled with a diagnosis of mental illness in their lifetime may choose not to have another label associated with who they are. Unfortunately, this is a misnomer, and some need professional help. You will not be able to dance it away, shout it away or even preach it away in church. Hear me good....... You just might need professional help. God wants you to be whole. The only thing wrong with professional help is not seeking it when needed. I totally believe God is the ultimate healer because professionals only treat the symptoms.

My road to becoming whole would require a supernatural intervention. As a young girl, I recall my family embracing what I know to be the Israelite culture.

Our Sabbath was Saturday and not Sunday. Some of the Jewish practices, such as not eating pork, not eating shellfish, and not doing any work until the sun went down, were my only takeaways. The exception was my grandmother Leanna Lee teaching us the twenty-third Psalm. I would often hear them talk about the God of Abraham, Isaac, and Jacob. The adults received the teachings while my siblings, cousins and I played in another room during the Saturday bible studies. I had limited understanding that a foundation was being laid without my knowledge.

My first introduction to Jesus Christ was attending a church service with my father and sisters on Easter. My only recollection is getting dressed up in nice clothes and receiving the Easter basket goodies. At the age of eighteen, I was formally introduced to Jesus Christ by Reverend Buford at "The Way of Christ MB Church." My best friend, affectionately known as Tori, invited me to her church. I remember the preacher singing this song at the end of the service. "There is Room at the Cross for You." My feet starting walking toward the altar. I gave my life to Christ and was baptized. Imagine being taught a different religion and now enters "Christianity." This is where the road to being made whole begun.

One Friday night the church had a guest speaker. As I sat in the back of the church towards the door, I was baffled. The preacher was laying hands on people and praying for them. He then proceeded to prophesy (I had no idea what that was) to a few people and started to speak in some strange language (heavenly language, what on earth is that?). Without any knowledge of the laying on of hands, speaking in unknown tongues and the prophetic, I left the service. I said to myself, "These people crazy; I am not going back there!" Instead, I went to the club.
I know right, the club! I left the church and went stepping at a club called Chic Ricks.

As I sat at the bar and ordered a drink, I heard someone say, "What in the world are you doing here? This is not where you belong." I now understand the Lord was speaking to me when I did not realize that I could hear his voice. Unfortunately, I walked away from the church and did not return until I was thirty years old. Even though I walked away, God had my friend Tori interceding for me.

I knew in my heart something was missing in my life. I did not know what that *something* was. We spend our lives trying to plug up the hole in our heart. We resort to serial relationships for affirmation or validation. We self-medication with drugs or alcohol. We pursue as many degrees as a thermometer. The journey to wholeness is building a relationship with God. We were created to worship Him. When we do not understand the purpose of something, we can misuse or misappropriate it. Cars were designed to run on fuel. If you continued to drive the car and not put any additional fuel in it, the engine would lock.

The car would be damaged. When we pursue every other relationship possible over a relationship with God, we will remain in a damaged state. He created us in such a magnificent way. The designer (God) put His name on us and created us in His image and His likeness for His glory. The bible declares in Isaiah 43:7 (KJV), *"Even every one that is called by my name: for I have created him for my glory, I have formed him; yea, I have made him.* You have been handcrafted, hand-picked, and created for His glory, created for His honor, and created for His praise. When you know who you are and whose you are, you will show forth His praises, realizing you are a designer's original.

Broken, can present itself in many forms: broken family relationships, broken friendships, being held back professionally because of race or gender, feelings of condemnation with being a single parent, and feeling alone are just a few. At the age of twenty-one, I now have a second child out of wedlock. The news of the pregnancy was devastating. My heart was broken at the thought of having a second child. Without knowing what the scripture said about fornication, I knew I did not want several children and not be married. After having my son, I decided that I would not be a lady with multiple baby daddies. We only know what we know. We do not know what we do not know unless we are taught something different. I did not realize this declaration would be life changing for me. Luke 12:48 states, *"But he that knew not, and did commit things worthy of stripes, shall be beaten with few stripes. For unto whomsoever much is given, of him shall be much required: and to whom men have committed much, of him they will ask more."* This verse simply means if we do what we want to do knowing that it is wrong, as opposed to being ignorant (not knowing), our punishment is greater when we know the truth and ignore it.

My broken heart was not only related to the thought of becoming pregnant. I discovered that I was pregnant after enrolling into Olive-Harvey College to pursue a career in nursing. My emotions were completely out of control during pregnancy. I felt like I was never going to be able to accomplish my goal to become a nurse. My young, twenty something year old brain wanted me to believe my life was over. Oh no, you have messed up yet again. My brokenness led me to consider putting my son up for adoption. I did not believe that I could manage two children when I was just entering the "alleged" adult phase of my life. When hearing of my potential decision, my natural father stated, "We don't do that." Wait a minute, what do you mean? The decision seemed like a reasonable conclusion, as abortion was never even considered. After the delivery, I suffered from what I now know was postpartum depression. My post-partum depression was undiagnosed and untreated, which eventually led to a severe suicidal attempt. Even though I went to school and became a Licensed Practical Nurse after my second son's birth, the depression did not mysteriously disappear. Instead, the depression was masked by educational accomplishments and training others as I bled inside. The enemy will try to destroy you before you know who you are in God. Jeremiah 29:11 (NIV) says, *"For I know the plans I have for you, declares the Lord, plans to prosper you and not to harm you, plans to give you a hope and a future."*

The plan was set to take my life, but God... I still remember the day and the hour. While at work, I met this guy who was an exterminator for the nursing home. He invited my friend and I to attend a musical at his church. I replied, "I ain't coming to no church, and as a matter of fact, you can call this number tomorrow and offer my mother your condolences."

I took my children to my mother's house and informed her I would be working a double shift the next day. My mother would watch the boys when I worked overtime. I returned home and turned on the television. As I sat and watched "The Cosby Show" every five minutes I would swallow ten Valium at a time. The last number I remember was forty. The exterminator called my mother that same night. He told her he was trying to reach me. I was not answering the phone. She told him that I might have turned my phone off because I was working a double shift the next day. He begged her to send someone over to see about me and verbalized his concern to her. At the time, I lived in a high rise called Lawless Gardens and you had to be buzzed in by security. My mother sent my brother over to check on me.

As the story unfolds, I was found on the floor at the side of my bed, barely breathing. My brother scooped me up and drove me to Michael Reese Hospital. He did not call 911 nor wait for an ambulance, which potentially saved my life. God used the exterminator and my brother as a vessel to thwart the hand of the enemy. The trap was set; however, the foundation had already been laid, and I belonged to God.

Today, as you are reading this book, know that the Almighty God has a plan for your life to give you not only hope but a future. The enemy may recognize who you are before you become. But rest assured, the devil has already been defeated, and his future is sure. My experience of brokenness was designed to fix someone else that might be struggling with depression or thoughts of suicide. The brokenness left me with a heart of compassion to want to see others made whole. The brokenness in the suicidal attempt and my behavioral health background helps me to recognize depression and assist individuals to navigate out of the dark place of depression. The brokenness was to assure someone reading this book that you do not have to stay where you are. There is help in the sanctuary and support in the behavioral health community as well.

As a Registered Nurse with a behavioral health background, I attest that mental illness is real and does not discriminate based on race, creed, and color. It is not taboo to seek help for any mental health issue you may be experiencing. It can be dangerous to ignore the signs. Well, how do I know the signs? Glad you asked. The symptoms of major depressive disorder (depression) are as follows, to name a few: little interest in doing things that once brought you pleasure, feelings of hopelessness as if things will never get better, trouble falling to sleep or sleeping too much, the lack of energy; poor appetite; overeating, considerable weight changes, feelings of failure, thoughts that you would be better off dead, and ideas to harm yourself.

My symptoms involved isolation and thoughts that my children would be better off without me. The enemy convinced me that my children would be well cared for by my mother. He failed to mention that this plan was not the will of God for my life. Professionally speaking, based on my height and weight and the amount of medication consumed, I should have been dead. BUT GOD! Instead, I now have the wherewithal through the Holy Spirit to recognize the demonic force of depression. My assignment is to cancel the funeral for someone else who may find themselves in the place I was delivered out of. God used the exterminator to rescue me, and I am here to rescue others.

Gone are the days of allowing the shame of a diagnosis to stagnate or immobilize you from seeking the help of qualified physicians. In many instances, we see in scripture where Jesus laid hands on the sick and they were healed of all their diseases. Other times, He sent His word and healed them from all their diseases. Again, there is help in the sanctuary and in the behavioral health clinic. Do not stay home and suffer in silence. We serve an omnipresent God (everywhere present at the same time). Just like He knew where I was, He also knows where you are. Today, I send the word of the Lord to you to consider, you might need professional help in addition to prayer.

After receiving counseling and medication management, the Lord healed me from depression. When I returned to work and to my family, the healing process continued. Attempting or taking your life is deemed as a selfish act or a cop-out. There is so much more to the diagnosis of depression that I would not learn until many years later. Depression affects the one struggling with the disease and those connected to them as well. Many of you feel that you know me personally and are reading this story's accounts for the first time. It is as painful to write as it is to remember. The goal is not to walk away feeling sorry for myself, but to heal so many others. Lord, make us whole.

Prayer: *Father, in the name of Jesus, we give you glory, honor, and praise. Thank you for being the giver and* *sustainer of life. Thank you for having us in your mind, before the sperm of our father ever met the egg of our mother. Thank you for knowing when we failed to know or understand, you had a plan and a purpose for our lives. We come against every demonic force of hell that would try to hold us captive to feelings of worthlessness, sadness, depression, and oppression. We decree and declare, whom the son has set free is free indeed. I decree and declare, Psalm 118:17 over our lives. "You shall not die but live and declare the works of the Lord." Lord you started a good work in us when you created us. Now Lord, perform your word over our lives. In Jesus' name I pray. Amen!*

_____

_____

_____

_____

_____

GRACEFULLY BROKEN

GRACEFULLY BROKEN

CHAPTER 5
THE PAIN HAS PURPOSE

In my opinion, every journey of brokenness was specific to the plan God had for my life. While we acknowledge He has a plan, we are also not ignorant of Satan's devices. If the enemy had all power and God did not, I would not be here to pen these words. In the area of psychiatric nursing, we are taught strategies for handling conflict. African American women are stereotypically viewed as "confrontational." Let me enlighten you, all confrontation is not hostile. There are five components of confrontation. The components are avoiding, commanding, accommodating, compromising, and collaborating. Of these components we can utilize the strategy of commanding against any enemy of our purpose.

When you confront the enemy of your destiny and purpose, you cannot sit by and avoid developing a strategy to knock the giant down. You do not want to compromise with, collaborate with, or accommodate that level of foolishness. Instead, you utilize your ability to TALK, TALK, TALK, and as the teacher would say, "use your words." Your words are the word of God. The scripture says in 2nd Corinthians 10:4, *"the weapons of our warfare are not carnal, but mighty through God to the pulling down of strongholds; casting down imaginations, and every high thing that exalteth itself against the knowledge of God and bringing into captivity every thought to the obedience of Christ.* Preacher, what does that mean? Glad you asked. Our weapon is the word of God. The world does not fight fair. We do not physically fight and we do not use physical weapons to destroy the enemy of our purpose. We use our weapons in the word of God through prayer, decreeing and declaring the word of God, and fasting to combat the devil. We lasso in every thought, emotion, and impulse that goes against what God has already said about us. We speak what He said about us. When you prepare for war in the natural, you must be trained. A part of the training involves knowing who your enemy is and recognizing when the attack has been launched. The time to get ready is not when the war starts. Your preparation behind the scenes is for a performance on the stage and, in the end, "YOU WIN!"

In the background, my brokenness was preparing me to bind up the broken hearted. My deliverance from the spirit of suicide developed tools to proclaim liberty to those who are captive with depression, suicidal thoughts and even those struggling with mental illness. How could I fix what was broken in others? Because He not only called me to it, *but He also anointed me for it.* The bible declares in Isaiah 61:1-2 (KJV), *"The spirit of the Lord is upon me because the Lord has anointed me to preach the good tiding to the meek; He has sent me to bind up the brokenhearted, to proclaim liberty to the captives, and the opening of the prison to them that are bound".* I was made for this assignment. The crushing and brokenness produced the oil.

The word anoint means to "smear or anoint with oil." For the oil to be produced, it must go through a process. The process for making olive oil is lengthy and costly. The olives are selected and chosen, whether ripe or unripe. The olives freshly harvested are considered the best source. Oil made with ripe olives provides a more nutritional value. Next, the olives are washed, and your fingers are used to scrub away any dirt. The process moves to separation. The olive oil leaves are picked off, twigs removed, along with debris. The olives are then drained of excess water and do not have to be completely dry. The next step involves crushing the olives into a paste. The purpose of the crushing is to facilitate the release of the oil from the vacuoles.

The purpose of intricately describing the process of making olive oil is to help you understand how this natural process is like our spiritual process. When God has a plan and a purpose for your life, you may find yourself experiencing a similar process. He will handpick you in your unripe or ripe stage. The Lord proceeds to wash you in His word. You are as valuable as the olive tree He chooses you from. Jesus removes figs, twigs, and leaves that are not reflective of who He is creating you to become. He might even drain you through the process, but not thoroughly. He does this by getting you to submit to His will and not your will. Here is where the residue of the past is scrubbed off. Next, the journey involves being separated from the old you, from people, from places, and from things for His glory.

He does all of this and then crushes you. He knows how long of a process will be required to remove hurt, fear, rejection, depression, lack of faith, etc., to produce the oil of the anointing He is preparing to smear the oil on you. You should not want to avert this process. You cannot do it without the oil. Allow the spirit of unforgiveness, rejection, abandonment, poverty, and even abuse to be broken off your life. You are no longer a victim. The word of the Lord comes to you today to decree healing from areas that God allowed you to be gracefully broken in. The word of God is here to set you free to become what He said about your life "in the beginning."

Similarly, we need to understand that when we abort the process, we open the door for the same seeds to be planted into our children's lives. Unfortunately, our children might not understand why they are the way they are. How does a child develop low self-esteem at the age of five? Why are so many of our youth having an identity crisis? Could it be that the dysfunction, the unaddressed generational curses, and the areas of brokenness that were never healed have spilled over into the lives of our children? Please stop for a moment and reflect on taking inventory only. You have now entered Planet Fitness, "The

No Judgment Zone." I do not just want you to be healed, but my desire is for you to be whole. In the words of Jesus, "Do you want to be made whole?" You have a choice in the matter. You decide! Isaiah 10:27 says, *And it shall come to pass in that day, that his burden shall be taken away off of thy shoulder, and his yoke from off thy neck, and the yoke shall be destroyed because of the anointing.*

My pain was purposed to aid others in having yokes of bondage destroyed off of their lives because of the anointing on my life. God did not wait until I came into the knowledge of who He called me to be before demonstrating His hand in my life. He used the schoolteacher to highlight my gift of gab. God used my natural father's hurtful words to show me I had more in me than I realized. My dad was angry that I was pregnant. He was probably embarrassed, but mad because he saw my potential. God used the compassion and love of my mother to demonstrate God's love in deeds and not in words only. My mother also saw potential and her love helped me navigate the pain, embarrassment, and rejection.

On your journey through brokenness, you might experience pain you never imagined possible. I am blessed to be the mother of two males and one grandson. However, there are some women who struggle with not being able to have a child. Throughout scripture, we read about individuals who experienced the pain and shame of barrenness. Sarai took matters into her own hands and gave her hand maiden to her husband, due to the shame and pain of barrenness. However, God allowed what He had spoken and originally designed to come to pass despite Sarai and Abraham's lack of faith in what God had spoken. The vison came to pass when Sarah produced Isaac.

Earlier, I discussed the sisters Rachel and Leah. Rachel struggled with not being able to produce a child. She prayed to God and He opened her womb. Her pain was so intense, she told her husband, in Genesis 30:1 (KJV), *"give me child lest I die."* Leah's brokenness, by the rejection from her husband, drove her to praise God. Isaac's wife Rebekah, drove him to a prayer closet to ask God to open her womb. Rebekah produced Esau and Jacob. The pain had a purpose. When Naomi's husband died and then her two sons died afterwards, her pain had a purpose. Examine the brokenness in your life. Assess the areas that appear to be the most painful and look for the purpose. You are not alone. We have all experienced the pain of brokenness.

It is hard to see the purpose when you are knee deep in the pain. Why would someone hurt me like this? What did I do to deserve that? I thought they were supposed to love me. Why would God allow this to happen to me? What kind of God would allow something like this to occur? We must resist the urge to blame God when our painful experiences in life challenge our faith. The pain of losing three family members in one year could blind you from seeing the purpose behind such a major tragedy. The loss of a job and the canceling of unemployment benefits in a pandemic is not something you want to find purpose in. As a parent, watching your child become a teenage mother, a son incarcerated, or the death of a child, are not life events you reflect on and say, "This pain has purpose." What you can be sure of, is that the God of all comfort sees you and knows right where you are. He can handle every aspect of pain you will experience. You were handcrafted and built to last. He knows how much you can handle.

    In the year 2020, we were faced with a pandemic. The pandemic required us to wear mask to prevent exposure to the Coronavirus. We were encouraged to social distance by standing six feet apart, some transitioned to a work from home employment, while others were forced to provide home school for their children. The pandemic forced social isolation on many. The isolation reminds me of living through the blizzard in 1979 in the city of Chicago. The snow was falling relentlessly, the winds were howling, and the temperatures rapidly fell below freezing. Sheets of ice developed that affected our ability to navigate the pathways. In some cases, we were as confined to our living quarters as we are in a pandemic. Yet, for a shorter time frame. The effects of prolonged isolation can take a toll on many of us. Cabin fever, depression, loneliness, the lack of human contact and social isolation are a few of the challenges experienced. As you become inundated with news reports repeating the length of time the storm or pandemic is expected to last, you can grow even wearier. The truth of the matter is that some form of storms will arise in all our lives. Remember, the storm is temporary. It has a scheduled end date.

The obstacles that present do not have to define you. The pain of a terminal diagnosis, the report from a physician stating death is imminent in a loved one or losing everything you have worked hard for in life can be challenging. The difference is when we understand the scriptures we can navigate the crisis knowing that trouble will not last always. You use your words to help you move from pain to purpose. What do you mean, use your words? Glad you asked. The word of God is present for every challenge we will ever face in our lives. We do not have to roll over and pull the covers over our head in defeat. As I stated earlier, we use our words as a weapon to defeat the enemy (the inner me).

The Lord told us to put Him in remembrance of His word. We use our words to speak the truth, and not the facts. The fact is, you do have breast cancer. The truth is, with His stripes you are healed. The fact is, you do not have enough food to feed your family until the day of your next paycheck. The truth is, the scripture tells us in Philippians 4:19, *"And my God will supply all your need, according to His riches in glory by Christ Jesus."* The fact of the matter is, you received notice that your family member has died. The truth of the matter is spoken in 2 Corinthians 1:3-5, *the God of all comfort is there to comfort you in all tribulation.* I will never attempt to make light of anyone's pain, but I want to assure you that God knows exactly where you are in the process and the pain has a purpose.

    You could not have told me in my teenage and young adult years, that the pain of rejection, feeling abandoned by my father, becoming a mother at a young age and growing up in the Harold Ickes Housing Project had purpose. The rejection was designed to direct me. The abandonment was to teach me that I was accepted in the family of God. The young mother who grew up in what some would call an impoverished area, taught me discipline, compassion, and drive to pursue the greater. Destiny and purpose can collide at any time and in any place.

The housing development I grew up in was a close-knit community. I grew up in a time when if a child was acting up, another parent in the neighborhood could discipline the child. Do not try that today. I grew up in an area of love that was so strong that even though we no longer reside in the area and the buildings have been demolished; the foundation stands sure.

The Harold Ickes is affectionately known as "The Low End." My "Low End" family knew who I was then, and respect who I am now. The people in the community have trusted me at some of the most painful and broken experiences in their lives. As one who has eulogized many, married some and counseled others, my Harold Ickes family have been a pivotal aspect of my development as a minister of the gospel. As one of my friends was on her death bed, I asked her, "What would you like for me to do for you?" Her reply was earth shattering for me. She said, "Just keep loving me like you always have." She left this earth knowing that I did not stand in judgment, but I stood in love. When you have the capacity to love people where they are, they will trust you in broken areas of their lives.

Prayer: *Father In the name that is above every name, the name of Jesus, show us who we are in you. Lord, many are reading this book, thinking that their past mistakes hinder them from moving into their future. Lord, I decree and declare that not only will they receive your forgiveness, but that you will strategically walk them through forgiving themselves. We send condemnation back to the pit of hell, and we decree and declare complete wholeness in us all— nothing missing, nothing broken. We thank you for putting the pieces together, even now. Lord, Heal the little girl in us without a father figure. Heal the woman or man looking for love in all the wrong places. Heal the person with whom negative words have been spoken over their lives. Lord, bring us all into the new creature you have created us to be since the world's foundation. Lord, we decree and declare,* *the burdens are taken off our shoulders and the yoke off our necks. We thank you, Lord, that the yoke of poverty, depression, mental illness, rejection, brokenness, fear, doubt, and unbelief shall be destroyed because of the anointing.*

Father, we do not want to skip the steps in the processing phase. We know that you know what it will take for us to become oily for your glory. Crush us, mix us, separate us, and refine us until the oil comes up as a sweet-smelling savor in your nostrils. In Jesus Name, we pray and give thanks. AMEN!

This looks pretty, however the process was not comfortable.

GRACEFULLY BROKEN

GRACEFULLY BROKEN

… GRACEFULLY BROKEN

CHAPTER 6
MENTORS ARE IMPORTANT

One of the most significant acts of kindness, by God, in my life is mentorship. Throughout the process of being gracefully broken, He strategically placed some excellent mentors along the way. Often people and especially the enemy, can see more in you than you see in yourself. My first experience with mentorship was with two women who are no longer in the earth realm. Sylvia and Patricia were two of the most influential mentors in my teenage life. They taught young women like me through their experience and through mentoring. Sylvia reinforced the importance of education. She was a teacher at Lane Tech High School in Chicago, and she was a math genius.

These two ladies embodied integrity, humor, discipline, and living by example to many individuals who grew up in the Harold Ickes. While onlookers said, "can any good thing come out of the projects?" we were being developed as future leaders. We were not condemned for mistakes we made along the way but challenged to not allow the mistakes to define us. They instilled the importance of education and principles for leading in a male-dominated environment. They celebrated our successes throughout our life and supported us in our failures. Yes, my mother instilled a lot in me, yet God saw fit to add a few mentors along the way.

Sylvia was a fantastic leader. I learned so much from her. The scripture says in 1Corinthians 3:7 (KJV), *"So then neither is he that planteth anything, neither he that watereth, but God that giveth the increase.* Mentorship allows us to view different perspectives. Like most teenagers, we think our parents do not know what they are talking about. We can hear the same principles from someone else and readily embrace the concept. She would provide raw truths and led by example. She was an educator, a mentor, and most importantly, she was a friend. Sylvia had no problem pulling your coat tail to get you back in order. Her sister Patricia was as instrumental in my development as she was.

Mentorship can manifest in many forms. Your ability to recognize mentoring is critical. Real mentors are not intimidated by who you are or who you will become. Instead of taking something from you, they impart into your life and bring something to the table for you to eat. Through the leadership of Sylvia and Patricia, I was able to recognize that teenage pregnancy was what I did but would not be how I was defined. God had a plan and a purpose for my life. I did not know all the details. Do not allow a misstep in life to leave you in a place of feeling the lack and capacity to recover. Keep showing up. Keep getting up. He has more in store for you. Keep moving forward and know that God gives us more while we are on our way to wholeness. Mentorship also came for me with a close friend with whom I grew up. Rochelle provided me with an opportunity to work at Walgreen's as a pharmacy technician. When the job ended, Rochelle said, "You should go to Dawson to become a nurse." She planted the seed. I went to school, the teachers watered the seed, and God gave the increase when I graduated as a Licensed Practical Nurse.

As a nursing student, I met several people who became more than colleagues. Some became mentors and others best friends. My friend/colleague Della and I met in nursing school. She was a Certified Nursing Assistant at the time. She entered nursing school with a particular skill set that I did not possess. She was instrumental in my development as a nurse during those formative years. When we graduated, we found ourselves working together at an extended care facility. While in orientation, I was trained by a nurse with a military background. She taught me organizational skills, integrity and helped me develop a keen eye for how to assess a patient.

While working at Warren Barr Pavilion, I met my next colleague and life-long friend Regina. I had no idea that our encounter would lead me to my next mentor. After one year on the job, I walked off the job. In the corporate world, this is called "job abandonment". I was angry that the supervisors would often send myself, Della and Regina to the skilled unit that was designed for registered nurses to work. I felt like they were dumping heavy assignments on us that we were not prepared to handle. My God, I was so wrong. I did not see myself as a Registered Nurse, but there were others who saw our potential. In my young twenties, I had no idea that the experience was orchestrated to further develop talents that were lying dormant.

Job abandonment and a recommendation from my friend Regina, led me to meet my next professional mentor. I was blessed to get a job at Michael Reese Hospital in a pediatric unit. After only six months on the job, the hiring manager came to me and said, "Toni, you need to go back to school and get your RN degree." I replied, "I am a single mother with two kids; I cannot afford to go back to school." She literally walked me through the process. She introduced me to tuition reimbursement, financial aid, and rotated my work schedule to accommodate my school schedule.

    I recall at a pivotal point in my life, while in nursing school, pursing a higher degree, working full-time and being a single parent, I fell in love. I had never experienced loving someone to this magnitude. My love for him lead to a broken heart. This experience left me feeling hopeless. When I look back, I can attribute the experience to another door of rejection that was forced open. With pain in my heart, I informed my mentor that I would not be going back to school. The enemy will make a fool out of you when you do not know who you are. One day, during my period of brokenness, I called off sick to work. Sandra showed up at my door. She listened attentively to my dilemma, allowed me to cry, and said, "You will go back to school, you will come back to work, and you will graduate." You see, she started as a ward clerk. She proceeded to earn a Bachelor of Science in Nursing and a Master of Business Administration. My process took on a similar journey. I went from becoming a Licensed Practical Nurse to an Associate Degree in Applied Science (Nursing) to a Bachelor of Science in Nursing. Amid a pandemic, I acquired a Master of Organizational Leadership Degree. Sandra remains a significant part of my life. I never hesitate to appreciate her for the affects her mentorship had on my life. My sisters, a few friends and others have attributed their journey to pursue a degree in nursing being based on my pursuit. People are watching your life. They may never say a word, but the impact could be tremendous.

My favorite story on leadership development is when I asked Sandra this question: "Why do you keep a uniform in your office?" She replied, "At times, it might get busy on the unit. I will take off my suit and put on my uniform and assist the staff." Today, I follow the same principle of being a servant leader. We should never get so high on our success that we forget our primary objective in life is service to others. It takes a form of humility as a leader to roll up your sleeves and get in the trenches with your team. She embodied the servant-leader.

It is absolutely no coincidence that God would lead me to obtain a degree in leadership. When you have received the gift of being trained under outstanding leaders, you owe it to others to pour the oil back into them.

Olives must be crushed to produce the oil. Leadership requires a significant amount of crushing before you fully develop. Yet, leaders are constant learners. As a lifetime student, I learned to give and provide feedback. However, I was not always good at receiving correction when I was younger. It took years for me to know that the feedback would one day make me a better leader. While you might not always like what the mentor or leader is saying, you must respect the fact that they have your best interest at heart.

One of the main components associated with leadership is influence. When I learned the principle of leadership, I realized we might not always like the person in authority, but we must respect the position. Leadership is about influence. You will not be able to receive the gift of mentorship if you are not willing to submit to leadership. As a good leader, you will have to learn how to compromise. The art of compromise develops your negotiating skills and keeps you humble. Each idea we have is not always the best idea. We must be integral enough to realize others on the team will possess insights and ideas that may be more effective. Now I will never advocate for going against what you believe. My suggestion is to remain true to who you are. Let us not win the battle and lose the war.

In my teenage years and in my professional career, I have learned from excellent leaders. My journey transitioned from personal leadership to professional leadership and to spiritual leadership. The foundation was laid at a young age and required me to remain open to being taught, and yes, corrected. People ask all the time if leaders are born or made. The answer is both. We are all born. However, our development as a leader requires work on our parts. We do not learn by osmosis. We learn through studying leadership gurus like John Maxwell. The principles of leadership work in every arena of our lives.

Now that I have discussed my professional mentors, I will navigate to my spiritual mentors. There is nothing like having a spiritual mentor. Spiritual mentors are as important as professional mentors. Spiritual mentors see in you what you have yet to see in yourself. They can push you to be the best version of yourself if you allow them the liberty. My first spiritual mentor and my best friend is

Pastor Tori, yet for me, she will always be Tori. She introduced me to Jesus at the age of eighteen. When I walked away from the church out of ignorance (not knowing and understanding), she never ceased to make mention of me in her prayers. Pastor Tori has been a constant mentor that has provided honest feedback, correction, and love at many junctures in my life. Tori remained steadfast and unmovable, always abounding in the work of the Lord. She taught me how to handle rejection, she taught me how to pray and she taught me how to stand on the word of God. The mentoring was not always with words but observed by watching her life in ministry. She always ascribed to the statement, "I won't move until God tells me to move."

Development in ministry is not for the faint at heart. Working in ministry requires you to work with people. When you work with people, you realize they bring the sum-total of who they are to the table. In ministry, we serve as volunteers and in most cases are not paid wages. Just think, when we are at work, we tolerate people for the purpose of receiving wages. However, in ministry, we commit to service as volunteers. In joining the army of the Lord, you would think that because we love God, this experience should be seamless. If you recall, I stated, "we bring the sum-total of who we are to the table." This means that while working with born again believers you will experience rejection, feeling of being ostracized, being misunderstood, or even being ridiculed while serving in the Kingdom of God.

God has a way of asking you to move in supernatural realms of uncharted territory. People might not always understand the call of God on your life. The call of God can make you move in a manner that is foreign to the onlookers. We see many instances throughout scripture to support leaders who were given unusual assignments. God told Abram, a paganistic worshipper (idol worshipper), to leave his country and his kindred and go to a land He would show him. This type of instruction takes faith. If you were not given the charge, you might find it strange. Jesus was a carpenter by trade. He instructed some fisherman to launch out into the deep and cast a net in an area that should not have fish. The fisherman had been out there trying to catch fish all night. Jesus used the power of influence to encourage the disciples to trust His word. It takes faith to move in the direction God is leading you, even when others lack the faith to see the vision. As a leader, you will experience a "nevertheless" attitude that says, "Nevertheless at thy word." People will not always understand your assignment, your anointing, or your call, but you must be like Nike and "Just Do It." Where God guides, He also provides.

At the age of thirty, my sister Stephanie recognized that I was going through a rough time and invited me to Lilydale Progressive M. B. Church. The pastor at the time, was the late Pastor Lawrence E. Mosley. He was an awesome man of God. Lilydale developed the foundation for my spiritual walk with the Lord through the study of the word of God. I would find myself every Wednesday night in prayer meeting with the saints of old. I remember vividly how Mother Patrick saw in me what I was unable to see within myself. One week in Sunday school, she told the class, Necie (my nickname) will be teaching the lesson next week. She did not confer with flesh (me). I was shocked. After the class, she came up to me in her quiet, calm demeanor and said, "Every week, you come prepared for the lesson. You can do this." And with His help, I did.

After the sudden unexpected death of Pastor Mosley, I transitioned to One Way Apostolic Church under the leadership of Pastor Noah Nicholson II. My introduction to this ministry was with an invitation from a friend to teach a CPR class. I had no idea at the time that the Lord was setting me up for a transition from Lilydale.

After the course, I felt the leading of the Lord to attend the church on the next two Sundays. I remember the pastor preaching a message, "The Past is Over." He literally preached my current situation of going through a divorce throughout the sermon. He did not know me from a can of paint. Lilydale was in mourning at our leader's unexpected death. There were so many other nuisances going on with his untimely death that a new environment was a welcome sight.

While at the now, Family Worship Center, the Lord continued to birth out what He had planted. God called me to preach the gospel in January 2000. Under Pastor Nicholson's leadership, I learned so much about leadership, serving in ministry, giving, ministering at different churches with different religious beliefs, and so much more. I have always been one with a grateful heart. On several occasions, I remind him that I am the woman of God I am today because of the seeds sown by his mentorship. I am exceeding grateful for everything he has taught me.

When I arrived at the church, I was also headed to divorce court. I came to the church broken, God used the preached word and the love of God demonstrated freely by the members of the church to heal my broken heart. You know you are healed when you are serving as a greeter and your ex-husband walks into the church with his new wife and you are not emotionally affected. I did say within myself, "out of all of the churches in the world, how did they come here?" Simply stated, they were invited by a colleague. God has a way of letting you know you are healed.

For sixteen years, the Family Worship Center assisted in my development in ministry. I was faithful, committed and served God and His people. This level of service and commitment did not come without its own level of brokenness. In my development, I made mistakes. I did not always speak peacefully to all men and women. The core of who I was had areas that needed to be broken. God used my new assignment to force me to look at areas in my life that needed to be changed. The pain was dormant. Yet, it was being magnified by my actions. God was using the gospel to change me, to correct me, and to instruct me. The love of a father will always bring correction. The first avenue God had to use to break me was "the word of God." I needed my will to be broken. I needed the stubbornness in my heart to be broken. I needed a heart free of pain and open to love to be transplanted into my life. God did this with the preaching and teaching of the gospel.

While serving in ministry, a new level of brokenness occurred. My experience involved those who rejected the call of God on my life based on my gender. Others with limited knowledge of who I was, rejected the gifts and talents God placed within me. There were also those who developed a perfect hate for me without knowing me. It took years to learn it was not me they hated. We have an enemy that comes to kill, to steal and to destroy our God-given purpose before we discover who we are in God. The enemy does not care who he uses to participate in the process. As you are in the discovery zone the enemy's assignment is to kill you before you arrive at the recovery zone. When you arrive at the recovery zone, you learn who you are and whose you are. This knowledge provides a level of confidence in God to assist you with caring less about the opinions of others.

In ministry and in the market-place mentorship can help aid you through the journey. Mentorship requires humility on the part of the mentee. Real mentors will never just tell you what you want to hear. They challenge you, they push you, and they even will get on your last nerve.

The mentor will provide insight based on getting to know you in the relationship. The mentor must be comfortable in providing feedback and the mentee must remain humble and receive the feedback as a mechanism to grow in the area they are being mentored. Some areas of brokenness can be prevented when we submit to the mentorship of our spiritual leaders.

As you walk in purpose and destiny, you should expect the enemy to come. Satan's job is to steal, kill, and destroy. He is consistent and his kingdom is not divided. Satan is relentless. As believers, we must stand girded with the whole armor of God. This military armor helps protect us in the fight. God told us the weapon would form. However, it will not prosper. We are not fighting against people, but people are used as a weapon in the battle.

After sixteen years at the Family Worship Center, the Lord directed me to my next level of spiritual mentorship. My transition was never planned but strategically orchestrated. I recall hearing in my spirit one Saturday evening, "Go to Bishop Hudson's church." I went to their 8:00am service because God is a God of order. Attending the early service would not interfere with my commitment to the Family Worship Center. Before visiting his church, I had several interactions with him in ministry, so the instruction to visit his ministry was not foreign. When I arrived, the intercessors were praying, and the power of God was undeniable. When the Bishop preached the message, I knew I had heard from heaven. Bishop William Hudson III preached until I found myself under the chair, on the floor in tears. I left there feeling God was healing my broken heart. You see, our church was in transition. The transition for me was painful. I felt the foundation under me had weakened somewhat, but I trusted God to deliver me.

When the second request was sent for me to visit Prayer and Faith Outreach Ministries, now the Powerhouse

Chicago, I honestly got nervous. Ok Lord, what in the world are you doing? Again, the Bishop preached until hell got the news that God set me up to be completely healed and set free. God was ordering my steps. My growth and development in ministry would now be stretched at a greater capacity. Archbishop William Hudson III is a phenomenal leader. He was born to develop and train leaders. He challenges and push leaders. He can move you to areas you did not even know existed, like writing this book. Amid a pandemic, in 2020, I have launched out into unchartered waters. The journey has landed me a new job at a diverse organization, completion of a Master Degree and with the mentorship of his wife Pastor Andria Hudson, to accept the call of God to walk in the office of a pastor. Recently, Pastor Andria Hudson challenged me in a session on "Passion and Purpose" to write two paragraphs to detail what a day in my life would look like if I walked in what I believed I am purposed for. This assignment pushed me to the depths of my soul, but I submitted and committed to the assignment. As a result, it was life changing and for that level of mentorship, I am eternally grateful.

He declared my end at the beginning.

Every leader needs a leader. We need people that will hold us accountable. We need leaders who will not just tell us what we need to hear, but leaders willing to challenge us when necessary. Ruth needed Naomi. Naomi needed Ruth. Elijah needed Elisha. Elisha needed Elijah. Moses needed Aaron. Aaron needed Moses. Let us not get so full of ourselves that we subscribe to our own press.

Leaders should apologize. Leaders should forgive. If you have hurt someone, wronged someone, or failed to pay a debt you know you owe, ask them to forgive you and make recompense. These simple truths could make a significant difference in your life. Do not dance over it, shout over it, or preach over it. God will hold you accountable as a leader. Ask me how do I know? He held me accountable.

As carriers of the gospel, we will not always get it right. However, it takes humility to admit when you are wrong. Arrogance is a huge problem in our nation. We need real leaders who are sold out for God and not just for themselves, their four, and no more. It is time for the Elijah's to rise and birth the Elisha's. Who are you imparting into? Who are you moving from a state of brokenness to a form of healing? We need to leave the place we departed better than when we came. To be made whole, we must acknowledge the broken areas in our life. How have the unhealed broken areas in your life affected how you lead the people assigned to you? SELAH.

Today, I move from brokenness to feeling like a message I recently shared, "Wilt thou be made whole?" And the answer is "yes". Yes, I consent to move from being broken financially to walking into a wealthy place. I agree to walk out of rejection into being accepted in the family of the beloved. Today, I walk out of the brokenness of word curses spoken over my life from people who were supposed to love me, into being set free by God. Today, I walk out of the brokenness of the shame of children out to wedlock to thanking God for blessing me with two sons and the best grandson on this side of heaven. Today, I walk out of the shame of divorce to knowing that He that has begun a good work in me shall perform it. Today, I am healed from the spirit of depression and suicide, and the joy of the Lord is my strength. My healing is a result of mentors that did not allow me to stay broken. They did not sugar coat the truth but challenged me to grow in every area of my life.

God is faithful. He keeps His promises. Moreover, He cannot lie!!! When you come to a juncture in your brokenness that you lose hope and fail to believe the words the Lord has spoken over your life; He will send a word of encouragement. At one of my lowest points, I received the most vital prophetic word in my entire life. The prophecy Archbishop Hudson spoke was so accurate that the enemy has come for it many times since the date of the prophecy. What amazes me about the Father is how He knows what concerns us concerns Him. Let me encourage you today. God has not forgotten what he promised you. He will hasten to perform His word. Serve Him while you wait.

As I conclude, let me encourage you. In serving the Lord and in your professional careers, the Lord will direct your path. Throughout the path, you will encounter mentors who will teach you what to do and what not to do. Mentors will challenge you. Mentors will get on your last nerve, irritate you and correct you. Ultimately, a true mentor will only want the best for your life. Your role as the mentee is to pursue the mentor as Elisha did with Elijah. Remain humble and submit to the authority as God develops you in every area of your life.

Prayer: *Father, in the name of Jesus, thank you for every professional and spiritual mentor that you have placed in our lives. Lord, forgive us when we failed to see what you were trying to show us through them. Help us to take what we have freely received and give it back to others. Most, if not all of us are where we are because of the sacrifice from mentors who saw in us what we could not see in ourselves. Lord, we thank you for their sacrifices. Lord, help us to forgive them that mishandled us in leadership. Lord, we ask that the residue of the pain, hurt, rejection, and disappointment be removed. In Jesus name, we pray AMEN!*

_____

_____

_____

_____

_____

_____

GRACEFULLY BROKEN

GRACEFULLY BROKEN

CHAPTER 7
THE BROKEN MOTHER

While the last chapter is encouraging, I must now focus on an area in my life that broke me the most. If you had to determine what you would consider the most painful place of brokenness that could take you out mentally, physically, emotionally, or financially, what would that be? As a parent, for me, it was my child. Well, he is no longer a child, but let me give you the backdrop as I hasten to a close on being gracefully broken.

My son was born in my senior year of high school, which means we grew up together. As a teenage mother, raising him with my mother's assistance, my dad, and my siblings was one of joy. Yes, it took a village, and my mother was the head of the town. Once my father laid eyes on him for the first time in the hospital, he was like a woman in travail. After I delivered my firstborn, my father was no longer in pain over his daughter becoming a teenage mother. My son is smart, friendly, and kind. Even as a young person, his cousins affectionately named him "Uncle Stank." He never gave me any problems growing up. He graduated high school. He did not get into legal trouble and has strong relationships with his peers and family. He loves basketball. His knowledge of the game and the history associated with the sport remains keen. I always thought he would become a sports analyst with his knowledge of basketball and football. He also has a good sense of humor.

When I told my son I was getting married, his response is one I will never forget. Unfortunately, I will not repeat in an effort not to offend anyone. But let us just say, he was spot on. Shortly after I got married, my son made the decision to move to Las Vegas, Nevada. He moved in with my sister initially. He later obtained a job and then secured his own apartment. During an election year in 1999, he worked on a campaign for a young man seeking a senate seat. He has always been one who connected seamlessly with people. The senator won his election, and here is where my youngest sister believed the issues began.

After the party, Anthony's life as we know it, would change forever. My sister called one day to tell me he was acting differently. He sat in the room, smoking cigarettes, and laughing inappropriately to himself. He was disheveled and neglecting his activities of daily living (bathing, grooming, cleaning up, etc.). When she and her husband visited his apartment, they discovered the apartment was filthy. After he came home in 2000, we did not know who he was. Without an initial clinical diagnosis, I was distraught with what I saw. I had no idea what happened to my son. To see the child I knew and loved, exhibit behaviors foreign to me, as his mother was devastating. Initially, I thought he was just on drugs. Some family members and even his father thought this was the issue and the reason for the changed behavior. Little did we know, this was only a band-aid on a soon to be gaping wound.

He checked himself into a hospital in Chicago and was transferred to Tinley Park Mental Health Facility for suicidal ideations (thoughts to commit suicide). He was officially diagnosed with Schizophrenia. While in the facility, he escaped from the Tinley Park Mental Health Institution and found his way back to Las Vegas without any financial resources.

Shortly after he returned to Las Vegas, my sister and her family moved to another state. All communication with my son ceased to exist and he was missing for at least nine years. For nine years, I did not know if he was alive or dead. At two junctures or so, in those nine years, he would call his grandfather and ask for thirty dollars. This was a consistent dollar amount he would request. Having not embraced a diagnosis of Schizophrenia, it was easier to believe it was drugs and not a mental illness. From 2001 until 2012 we only heard from him twice.

My brokenness left me feeling as if he were dead in a grave somewhere and I would never see him again. Every birthday, Mother's Day, and Christmas grew dim. On random occasions, I would call the prisons and once I reached out to the morgue. The experience was so horrific that I never called the morgue again. There were times when I stood firm in my faith and other times the heart of a mother would manifest. My heart seemed as if it was shattered into pieces. It is one thing to pray for a miracle for one year or even two years; however, when you start getting into five years, six years, or even seven years, you can lose hope. The bible declares in Proverbs 13:12 (KJV), *"Hope deferred maketh the heart sick"*. My heart was sick. I worked every day taking care of others and did not know if he was alive or dead. I remained faithful to serving in ministry and caring for patients while I was secretly and sometimes not secretly bleeding on the inside.

My nursing journey led me to Hartgrove Hospital to work in a behavioral health facility. A colleague insisted I would love working there. I told her I did not like psychiatric nursing when I was in school. Later, I decided to work part-time to earn some extra cash, so I thought. I was being set up. Hartgrove became my teaching ground for learning about the area of psychiatric nursing. In my humble opinion I met and worked with some of the best group of nurses, mental health workers, and program specialists in the business. They taught me the framework of behavioral health nursing. God allowed me to develop relationships with physicians, counselors, and social workers. I had no idea how much I would need their clinical expertise.

After nine years of my son being missing, I received a call from a police officer. He said, "We have your son here." My heart dropped, as I waited anxiously to hear what he would say next. He proceeded to say, "He is right here and wants to come home." My son arrived back in Chicago on the fourth of July (Independence Day). When I picked him up from the bus station after working nine years in behavioral health, I knew he was sick. He was elated to see me. I struggled to open my mouth. He sat anxiously laughing to himself and talking rapidly (pressured speech). His thoughts were disorganized, and he transitioned from one conversation to the next. He appeared to respond to the voices in his head. He had traveled twenty-four hours on a Greyhound bus from Las Vegas to Chicago. The body odor was pungent. As I drove in silence, I fought back the tears. Based on my newly obtained knowledge of mental illness, I realized my son looked like the patients I had spent the last nine years taking care of.

Based on my established relationships, I put systems in place to get him the help he so desperately needed. I had no idea the amount of stigma associated with mental illness until I was knee-deep in it, trying to find available resources. I was a mother attempting to answer questions that I had no answers to. Where did the illness come from? Whose side of the family was it associated with? Did someone put something in his drink during the inauguration party? How do you "get" Schizophrenia? I had more questions than answers.

According to the DSM V, the diagnosis Schizophrenia requires a person to meet a specific criteria. The criteria involved two or more symptoms for at least one month or longer. The symptoms are delusions, hallucinations, disorganized speech, grossly disorganized or catatonic behavior. The disturbance is not caused by the effects of a substance or another medical condition. Some associated features are inappropriate affect (laughing in the absence of stimuli). Schizophrenia is a chronic mental disorder involving a breakdown in the relation between thought, emotion, and behavior. This leads to faulty perception, inappropriate actions and feelings, withdrawal from reality, and personal relationships. Besides, some live with fantasies, delusions, and possess a sense of mental fragmentation. In simple terms, individuals with Schizophrenia hear voices that tell them to do things that could be dangerous, like taking their own lives. They have delusional thoughts, such as they may think they are the United States president, or the government is out to get them. Some experience a lack of emotion, withdrawal from relationships with family and

friends, and religiosity. Others may become stuck in a time machine. Most experience hallucinations or disorganized thoughts.

The symptoms are not all the same for each person diagnosed. In my son's case, he was homeless, living in and out of psychiatric facilities in Las Vegas and Arizona with no support system because of HIPAA which stands for the Health Insurance Portability and Accountability Act. By law, without his permission, they could not share if he were hospitalized and he lacked the capacity to provide consent. On several occasions, the police in Las Vegas refused to file a missing person's report stating he is an adult and might not want to be found. On a few occasions we learned he was incarcerated for panhandling.

Panhandling is described as people who walk up to a total stranger and ask for money. He described incidents in the shelters where individuals reported being physically or sexually assaulted along with having their personal belongings stolen. To paint the picture, it reminds me of those individuals living on Skid Row in Chicago. There are individuals living under over passes and bridges. They accumulate belongings and opt to live in what seems like horrific locations even amid frigid temperatures as opposed to living in a homeless shelter. Some individuals that live there are not on medication for their mental health issues. When we come across people asking for money (panhandling), we assume they want to buy drugs. In some instances, they might be hungry. Others use drugs to drown out the voices in their head. They might self-medicate with alcohol, marijuana or even crack cocaine to drown out the voices. To walk up to a stranger and ask for any type of assistance takes confidence. However, it is also dangerous, especially in Chicago. My fear was that people who saw him on the street would not arbitrarily view him as one with a mental illness because of his intellect and friendly personality.

When my son returned home, after getting him somewhat stabilized, he would share some of his experiences. Most are too painful to discuss. He would share stories that did not have any filter and were difficult to listen to while trying to keep a straight face. As one with a high intellect, his recall was vivid of the past. Often, it felt like he was stuck in a time capsule at age eighteen. He would talk about going to college and living on campus; however, he was thirty-five years old. He would verbalize wanting to lose his stomach, so he could try out for the NBA. This behavior is descried in the behavioral health world as delusions. As a behavioral health nurse, I witnessed some of these same behaviors in my patients. Some would attempt to call the White House to report a crime. Others focused on religiosity and had a strong grasp on the scriptures, yet disorganized thoughts prevented them from articulating the scripture in the correct context.

When I discussed me telling his story, he was supportive. He asked a lot of intelligent questions and provided dates and timelines that I purposely blocked out. The son I raised was respectful, funny, smart, and almost never was a problem to raise. When he would get out of line, I would make one phone call to his dad and not have any issues for several months. What broke me was when I was forced to learn who he had become with the disease. I wanted to blame the man who ran for senator, that was until I realized the disease is not drug or alcohol induced.

I learned that Schizophrenia presents in the mid to late twenties and his disease was evident by age 21. Men tend to experience symptoms earlier than women.

He was always close to his brother, cousins, and friends. To witness social isolation where he would only interact with them for short intervals and request to leave, was startling. His grandfather, his dad and I are the ones with whom he communicates. He also loves to call his maternal grandmother to discuss sports. Deterioration of personal hygiene, insomnia, extreme reaction to criticism were new and not attributes of the child I had raised. At times, he would become angry. He would yell, hang up the phone or use his famous line with me which is "I know you don't talk to those Christians like that." I would reply, "I thought you were a Christian," and he would laugh. He lacks the capacity to stay angry for any length of time and does not like arguments or confrontation. Yet there have been instances in some of the facilities that he resided in where he became angry enough to stand up for himself. My role shifted from being his mother to becoming his advocate.

He moved from state to state. I was forced to obtain medical guardianship. I did not want him to go missing again and I not be able to obtain any information due to privacy laws. I found myself constantly talking to multiple hospitals and doctors each time he moved to a new state because he thought things were not working out where he lived. He has never embraced the diagnosis and when upset he will say "I am only taking the medication for you because I don't need no medication." Coming to grips was challenging, but the issues after the diagnosis were more troubling.

In my discovery of the world of mental illness, I learned that Las Vegas does not have the mental health facilities that the state of Illinois has. In Las Vegas, entrepreneurs purchase homes and receive government funding to run an independent living facility. My encounters were with individuals who verbalized they provided services for those with mental illness. Countless locations would state they would provide medication management, behavioral health oversight, food, and housing. Instead, they manipulate individuals with disabilities and require eighty percent of their monthly social security check. The staff on hand are not professionally trained to deal with mental health issues. Some locations, per my son, were infested with bed bugs, roaches, untrained personnel, and limited supervision. In one facility in Las Vegas, Anthony shared with me how two people died due to heat exhaustion due to the owner rationing the air conditioning.

In January 2019, my sister Rachel and I decided to travel to Las Vegas to surprise my baby sister for her fiftieth birthday (her family moved back). On day two of our trip, we went to visit my son who had also returned to Las Vegas. I was devastated at what I witnessed. (Talk about feeling broken). My son was dirty, smelled awful and based on my clinical assessment was not properly medicated. He was excited to see us, but his only request was for thirty dollars. When I went to look at his living quarters, I could have thrown up. The room consisted of three (yes three) twin sized beds in a room for adult males. When my sisters and I returned to our room, I cried for an extended amount of time. My family felt my pain but felt as helpless as I did, in most instances.

There are two people who shared this tremendous pain with me. My son's father and my dad. We have grieved the loss of the child we knew and loved. He had now become someone we would have to learn to get to know. While some things had changed, there were some things that remained the same. His love for us was evident, even when he would get upset. His sense of humor remains intact. He consistently talks about "buying me a church." He uses terminology like "sister girl, I'm gone buy you a church." He verbalized wanting to have a girlfriend and a baby like his brother. When he assesses his cousins' lives, he is conscious of not having a driver's license, not having a job, and not having any children. With a high intellect, he has obtained several jobs throughout his mental illness. However, once he worked for a few days, the managers recognized something different about him. He could not understand why he could not take as many smoke breaks as he wanted. He would become frustrated and quit the job. When he set a goal, he would endure the rules of the organization. For example, once, while living in Chicago, he worked at Applebee's. He was employed long enough to make enough money to buy a ticket to return to Las Vegas.

He literally called me from the airport, stating he was going back to Las Vegas because it was too cold in

Chicago. How did he purchase the ticket? He does not have a credit or debit card. Again, his intellect remains high, but his insight and judgment remained poor. When Las Vegas temperatures became too hot, he returned to Chicago. The financial losses, the emotional turmoil, the concern for his safety and the grief over my son, as I knew him, broke me the most. The stress started to take a toll on me. My family could not help me because they did not understand. High school friends and some family members disconnected from him. He would ask family members, friends, and complete strangers to send him thirty dollars for cigarettes. When they declined, for whatever reason, he would get angry and recall how he helped them in the past. He has the heart of a giver, which is like that of his mother. Unfortunately, with the disease, he lacks insight and judgment.

As a mother, my son's diagnosis seemed as though it was the most horrific area of brokenness. During a recent conversation with him, I told him to make sure he wears a mask in the community and to socially distance himself from others. Because of the pandemic, my fear was in his random approach to strangers he could be assaulted, seen as a threat, or get the virus. After all, he is an African American male who prefers to approach individuals who do not look like him to ask for money. He has no understanding of the effects of COVID 19. When I discussed fatalities related to the disease, his reply was true to his character. He replied, "Mom, I am not afraid to die, because I know when I die, I am going to heaven."

He joined Lilydale MB Church at the age of seventeen and was baptized, while in his right mind. The foundation was laid. When he returned home one day, we were discussing his desire to "buy me a church" and he said, "I know I am saved, I am just worried about a few other people getting to heaven." We both laughed ecstatically at those whom he named.

Most of you reading this book, might not be aware of the struggle in caring for a person with a mental illness. Let me share with you, it is not for the faint at heart. God in His infinite wisdom prepared me when I did not recognize that I was being prepared. Why would He allow me to go through so much pain? He was crushing the olive, to obtain the oil. Imagine the feeling of getting a call from a social worker that you worked with to inform you that your son has been admitted to the hospital on the same nursing unit you worked on. The thought of visiting on the unit brought on additional stressors of the shame associated with mental illness. The good news is my friends and colleagues at Saint Mary and Elizabeth hospital treated me like I had treated so many other families, with love and compassion.

Often, we look at pain as a strange bed fellow. We fail to assume the position that pain has a good purpose. We shutter at the thought of any area of brokenness having good to come out of something that seems so mortifying.

The pain pushed me in my prayer life. The pain pushed me in my study of the word of God. The pain pushed me to a new level of compassion. The pain restored some relationships, strengthen others, and disconnected many. People look at our life on the outside and form an imagery of what our life is like. Truthfully speaking, if it were up to me, there is no way I would have shared my story with this level of transparency. However, we cannot conquer what we are unwilling to confront. I was forced to research the root of the disease.

It has taken years to find out that mental illness went back through several generations undiagnosed and untreated on my mother's side of the family. I had to discover the root of the disease so I would know how to fight in the spirit so that this disease would not continue in our blood line. Mental illness is real. It was time for me to "use my words." I am reminded of the story in the bible about a woman who went to Jesus and asked him to heal her daughter who was "grievously vexed with a devil." The individual seeking assistance was first a woman. Secondly, she was a Gentile and not a Jew. In this space of time women were second class citizens. In biblical days, women did not approach men in public. Not like you jokers today! Laugh and move on. Mark 7:24-30 (KJV) says, *Then Jesus went thence, and departed into the coast of Tyre and Sidon, and behold, a woman of Canaan came out to the same coasts, and cried unto him, saying, have mercy on me, O Lord, thou son of David; my daughter is grievously vexed with a devil. But he answered her not a word. And his disciples sough him saying, Send her away; for she crieth after us. But he answered her and said, I am not sent but unto the lost sheep of Israel. Then she came and worshipped him, saying, Lord, help me. But he answered and said, it is not meet to take the children's bread, and cast it to dogs. And she said, Truth, Lord: yet the dogs eat the crumbs which fall from their master's table. Then Jesus answered and said unto her, O woman, great is thy faith: be it unto thee even as thou wilt. And her daughter was made whole from that very hour.*

There are so many messages is this passage of scripture. This woman risked her life to reach out to Jesus on behalf of her sick child. As a woman and as a Gentile, she could have been stoned to death. However, her faith and desperation on behalf of her sick daughter led her to the feet of Jesus. She took on a posture of worship which takes humility. She fell at His feet, she acknowledged that He is Lord, and even when insulted by Jesus remained humble and relentless in her request. Most of us would have lost it. Once he implied you were a dog, many of us would have missed our miracle. I have a few questions for you to consider. How bad do you want it? What are you willing to give up for the miracle you are requesting? Last but certainly not least, what if the response is not the answer you were looking for?

Life has dealt me a hand that I wanted to fold. In the process of being gracefully broken, I learned to trust the process. One of the processes for me was when God told me to write Anthony's obituary. He then proceeded to show me in the scripture. He showed me how David fasted and prayed waiting on God to heal his son. His son died. David did not get the request he made. When his son died, David got up, washed his face, changed his clothes, ate some food and went into the temple to worship the Father. The Lord spoke in my spirit and said, "Let the enemy know that if I decide to take Him, you are still going to praise me." The amount of freedom I received after following the instructions was refreshing. You see, at the time of the request I was being tormented with the thought of my son lying in a pauper's grave and never seeing him again. BUT GOD!!!! My son is still here.

Prayer: *Lord, we come in the name of Jesus on behalf of every mother struggling with a missing son or daughter, on behalf of every parent struggling with caring for a child with mental illness, and on behalf of any parent struggling with grieving the loss of a child as they know it. Lord, we send a word of healing to each of us. You were wounded for our transgressions. You were bruised for our iniquities. The chastisement of our peace was upon you and with your stripes we are healed. Heal every broken mother. Heal every broken father. Heal the broken grandparent, heal the broken siblings. Give us the garment of praise for the spirit of heaviness. Lord, if the situation does not change, give us peace. In Jesus name, we pray, AMEN!*

_____

_____

_____

_____

_____

_____

GRACEFULLY BROKEN

GRACEFULLY BROKEN

CHAPTER 8
AND WE KNOW

The bible declares in Romans 8:28 (KJV), *"And we know that all things work together for good to them that love God, to them who are called according to his purpose."* One thing I am crystal clear on is "He called me." He called me before the sperm connected with the egg. He called me knowing every obstacle in life I would face. He called me knowing that even after I had given my life to Him, I would still mess us, and yet He not only called me but chose me in Him before the foundation of the world. One of my favorite passages of scripture, as it relates to the broken areas I have experienced, is found in Romans 5:1-5 (KJV) and reads, *"Therefore being justified by faith, we have peace with God through our Lord Jesus Christ: By whom also we have access by faith into this grace wherein we stand and rejoice in hope of the glory of God. And not only so, but we glory in tribulations also: knowing that tribulation worketh patience; and patience, experience; and experience hope: and hope maketh not ashamed; because the love of God is shed abroad in our hearts by the Holy Ghost which is given unto us.* You see, all the broken areas had to happen. SELAH!

The relationship tribulation had to happen. The financial challenges had to happen. The assaults on my character and integrity had to happen. The harsh words spoke over my life had to happen. The diagnosis of my son had to happen. Wait, you must be crazy. This did not have to happen. When you understand scripture, you see throughout history most, if not all the characters in scripture experienced tribulation.

If you recall, I started with Leah and Rachel. However, allow me if you will, to go back further and do a quick roll call. Adam and Eve disobeyed God and lost their place in paradise. The Lord knew the choice they would make and had already made provision. Adam and Eve suffered the death of one son, by his own brother (tribulation). Moses killed a man and was chosen to lead to the children of Israel (tribulation). The very people he was called to lead, lost confidence in him and made idols to worship instead (tribulation). Noah built an arch after being instructed that it was going to rain at a time when no one had seen rain. He was mocked while working to complete his assignment. Yet, even after completing the assignment, he found himself drunk and his nakedness was uncovered (tribulation). Abram and his wife Sari wanted a child. Sari was barren and decided to take matters into her own hands and give her hand maiden to her husband to produce a child. The only problem was the Lord had already promised them a child. Many of us have taken matters into our own hands when the promise did not occur within our time frames (tribulation). To add insult to injury, when the child was born, now you have the wife and the handmaid at odds with one another (tribulation). God kept His promise, despite Abram and Sari's decision. I find it interesting to note that their promised seed produced two children (Jacob and Esau) who started a fight in the womb. I am sure by now you get the picture.

If you go back to the beginning, you will see what we call "first mentions." Tribulation did not just arrive at my doorstep because I am some great wonder. It started with my ancestors in the garden when sin entered. Romans 5:19 KJV says, f*or as by one man's disobedience (Adam), many were made sinners, so by the obedience of one shall many be made righteous (Jesus)*

I want to encourage you to stop beating yourself up with the tribulation you have or are experiencing. The tribulation is working for your good. Tribulation worketh (*eth* is a continual process) patience. You will learn to wait on God in the tribulation, to trust God in the tribulation and to acquire patience. Let me be honest and say that throughout the time of not knowing whether my son was alive of dead, I did not always stay in faith.

GRACEFULLY BROKEN

To be gracefully broken, would require my faith to be challenged. The bible declares in Proverbs 13:12 (KJV), *"hope deferred makes the heart sick, but desire is fulfilled as a tree of life."* My heart was sick, yet when he returned home, the desire produced a tree of life. How can you say that when he returned with a mental health diagnosis? I can say this because my prayer was to not allow him to die and be buried in a pauper's grave and I never know where he is. While the prayer was answered, it had tribulation attached.

My heart ached as a mother, but I was no longer paralyzed. You see, many who know me will be reading this testimony for the first time. Yes, I really do not look like what I have been through, but it is only by the grace of God. I rest in the fact that as his mother and as his advocate, I have done everything humanly possible for him. And having done all, I stand in the confidence that God will perfect that which concerns me, and everything attached to me.

In relationship to ministry, while word curses were spoken, they were like the kiss Judas gave Jesus. The purpose was to push me to my destiny. The rejection by those who were supposed to love me, developed a tenacity that cannot be denied. In the voice of Noel Jones, the rejection was direction. We can become stagnate and complacent. We might just need the nudge of a Judas in our lives to shift us into the original designed destination God has in store for us. The rejection should make us better and not bitter. We should not use our words or inside information we are privy to, to hurt people that have only helped us. If you have an ought with someone it is only right to go to that one individual and attempt to get the situation worked out if possible. We must surmise, some might not want to reconcile. Here is where we shake the dust off our feet.

By nature, I have a bit of stubbornness within. This attribute is not a bad one to have when placed in the right context. The stubbornness pushed me to pursue higher education. He encouraged me to challenge issues I was passionate about, yet at the same time it caused problems when God was trying to break areas in me as it relates to leadership. Leaders are strong willed. Leaders are visionaries and can see it before it manifest. Leaders have structure and discipline. The trait which required development was "personality." I am a serious person most of the time. I love to laugh and have fun, but only when the job is done.

This is a problem. When people look at your face and deposition and see only a serious disposition, you are labeled as "unapproachable." There is some truth in this assessment, but not all truth. When you are serving in leadership, the people you lead have no idea what issues you are facing. While they are judging the lack of friendliness, they do not get to see that the cut you applied a Band-Aid to, has become a gaping wound. Underneath the surface, the wound is now gangrene, odorous, and in need of an amputation because the cells are no longer receiving oxygen (I know you thought I forgot), but you continue doing everything within your power to show up to the church, show up to the job, and even show up for your family, while oxygen is being depleted behind the scenes.

Let me encourage you by saying, I went from barely being able to breathe and consistently showing up, to receiving the joy of the Lord as my strength. I am happier at this age and stage of life than I have ever been in my life. I made a choice. I chose me. I chose to control what was within my scope of practice and leave the remainder to Jesus. My tribulation has worked patience, my patience has worked an enormous amount of experience and my experiences regardless to how horrific have worked hope. This hope is one I am not ashamed of. Philippians 1:6 (KJV) says, *"Being confident of this very thing, he that hath begun a good work in you will perform it until the day of Jesus Christ."* God is not finished with me. I remain a work in progress. His love, compassion and mercy has been consistent, and I am fully persuaded He will complete what He started.

Prayer: *Father in the name of Jesus, thank you for choosing me. Thank you for loving me. Thank you for allowing me to complete the degree program, thank you for allowing me to complete the book, thank you allowing me to complete the purchase of a home, thank you for blessing me to get a new job during a pandemic with financial increase, thank you for blessing me to learn behavioral health nursing so I can advocate for my son. Thanks for keeping my heart and mind through Christ Jesus. Thank you for seeing in me what others have yet to discover. My prayer is that you would bless every person reading this book to receive your love, your forgiveness, your deliverance and your blessings. Bless their faithfulness to you. Teach them to make their request known unto God.*

Lord we decree and declare not only will you heal those reading this book, but that you would make them whole. In Jesus name, Amen!!

GRACEFULLY BROKEN

GRACEFULLY BROKEN

GRACEFULLY BROKEN